BEYOND THE CALL OF DUTY

Heart-warming stories of canine devotion and wartime bravery

ISABEL GEORGE

HarperElement
An Imprint of HarperCollins*Publishers*
77–85 Fulham Palace Road,
Hammersmith, London W6 8JB

www.harpercollins.co.uk

and *HarperElement* are trademarks of
HarperCollins*Publishers* Ltd

First published by HarperElement 2010

This production 2013

© Isabel George 2010

Isabel George asserts the moral right to be
identified as the author of this work

A catalogue record of this book is
available from the British Library

ISBN 978–0–00–737151–8

Printed and bound in Great Britain by
Clays Ltd, St Ives plc

MIX
Paper from
responsible sources
FSC™ C007454

FSC™ is a non-profit international organisation established to promote
the responsible management of the world's forests. Products carrying the
FSC label are independently certified to assure consumers that they come
from forests that are managed to meet the social, economic and
ecological needs of present and future generations,
and other controlled sources.

Find out more about HarperCollins and the environment at
www.harpercollins.co.uk/green

*To my parents who showed, by example, that
courage, loyalty and love really can conquer all*

ISABEL GEORGE was born in Shropshire, where her family encouraged her early passion for animals and history. A degree in English and History opened a door to the public relations department of veterinary charity PDSA.

Isabel's interest in animals giving loyal service to the Armed Forces began with her father sharing stories of the Royal Navy mascots he met in his twenty-five years in the Senior Service. Not all of the stories had a happy ending, but all told of the unique bond that exists between service men and women and their animal companions in times of peace and conflict.

Isabel now lives in Shropshire with her three children, two hamsters and an almost-human Jack Russell, fox terrier cross called Scrumptious.

Contents

Smoky –
A Dog with a Destiny

'Smoky was a diversion from the demoralizing reality of the Pacific War. She made us laugh and forget. The thought that it could all end suddenly was all too sobering. So, as we flew together on combat missions, I was ready for the worst but remained determined, within all my power to keep her safe. We were a team.'

(William A. Wynne – from his memoir, *Yorkie Doodle Dandy*, published by Wynnsome Press)

Miracles probably happen every day but few are witnessed and many more go unrecorded. Why? Because they just 'happen'. But in a theatre of war where miracles are rare, they shine bright. Here, in the fearful darkness of hostility, where good stands out so clearly from bad, a miracle, however small, is something to treasure in memory – forever.

When Bill Wynne first laid eyes on Smoky he wasn't exactly sure what he was looking at. Standing a little closer, the tall, dark, handsome GI from Ohio could just about make out that the baseball-size mass of brown fur in front of him had four short legs, two beady black eyes, and a leathery little nose but beyond that, its true identity was a mystery.

'What kind of beast is this?' Bill asked, turning to an oil-soaked Sergeant Dare. Blinking in the sunlight as he emerged from under the chassis of a Jeep, Dare confessed that he hadn't a clue. All he knew was that Ed Downey had found the little thing in a foxhole in the jungle and then dropped it back with him at the 5212th Photographic Wing motor pool along with his vehicle. After giving Dare the lowdown on the unreliable Jeep that had been assigned, Downey offloaded his jungle 'find'.

'Hey, Dare, I found this in a foxhole,' he said, thrusting the mass of brown fuzz into the sergeant's greasy hands. 'This damn thing broke down,' he said banging his fist against the olive metal, 'and in the sudden quiet I heard a yelping sound and at the end of it – this. I don't know what it is but I know I don't want it.' Downey walked away towards his tent, frustrated by the day, the unreliable vehicle and the overpowering, wet heat of the New Guinea jungle.

Sergeant Dare already had enough to do in the motor pool. He didn't see himself adopting this animal but he knew a man who just could be this creature's salvation. In the meantime, he offered the animal water and food and, to help it cool down, he grabbed the hand shears and hacked away some of its excess hair. Frightened, near-scalped but still smiling and hopeful, the strange sweet thing fixed its gaze on the man standing in front of him who was wearing the puzzled expression.

Bill Wynne had been told about Dare's new house guest and had wandered over to take a look. He squatted down for a closer inspection and got more than he bargained for – a big, wet, lick on his face. 'Well it's a dog,' said Wynne, 'but it looks kind of weird thanks to the haircut and I'm not sure it's healthy. Where did you say you found it?'

The sergeant repeated the story and said that three Australian dollars would clinch the deal. Money wasn't the problem. In US terms, that was around $9.66. What Bill didn't want to do was become emotionally attached to this crazy-looking dog and then have it die on him a short time later. Bill's twenty-one years of life had already been filled with more than his fair share of sadness. He had become accustomed to losing those he loved and he wasn't in a rush to go through anything like that again. He had a feeling that nature might take its course with this fragile little life and made up his mind to wait until morning before parting with the three dollars.

Bill prayed that the little dog would make it through the night. They had only met briefly but there was a part of him that admired her spirit. Dare's story had tugged on his heartstrings and there was an immediate empathy with a fellow creature that was also caught up in the uncertainty of the war and all its horrors. One thing puzzled Bill more than anything he had heard so far: how on earth had she ended up in the jungle in the first place? He marvelled at the miracle that caused Ed Downey's Jeep to break down at that exact moment and in that precise location where the dog's cries could be heard. But the string of miracles didn't stop there. The biggest of all the dog's lucky breaks was that Downey picked her up at all. He didn't like dogs and didn't mind admitting it, but he still followed the sound of the cries, rescued her and took the lost pup back to base. If none of that had happened, the animal's life would probably have been snuffed out by heat exhaustion, starvation or one of a variety of predators which included the native tribes. But her life wasn't taken and she seemed determined to live. Thanks to a series of fortunate events and happy coincidences, the small creature's life was just about to begin.

The next morning Bill's prayers were answered. Smoky was no longer a sickly looking beast peeping through the stumpy chunks of a bad haircut. The dog that Dare had called Smokums was a real survivor. Less than twenty-four hours earlier she had been pacing and weaving with anxiety and looked as though the trauma of it all might break her. But no. Thanks to Dare feeding her up and giving her a comfortable bed for the night, Smoky had defied the odds stacked against her and could now relax into her good-natured, loveable self. Bill handed Dare the new asking price of two Australian dollars. As the Sergeant pocketed the money and dashed back to his card game, Bill tucked Smoky under his arm and headed for his tent.

It was lucky for everyone that Smoky was only seven inches tall at the shoulder and four pounds in weight. A larger animal companion would have stretched the minimalist accommodation way beyond the possibility of comfort. The tent had room for the bare essentials only: a cot bed to sit, sleep and eat on and stacking space for storing regulation-issue kitbags and contents. The old expression, 'Not enough room to swing a cat' could have been adapted to, 'Not enough room to swing a tiny Terrier'. Pitched row upon row on cut grass the tents made up the Wing camp area. Each tent had its own foxhole directly outside so the men could dive for cover during raids and beyond the tents was the high grass leading to jungle and the mountains beyond. The view from Wynne and Downey's tent was jungle. Dense, green and totally alien to the US Forces stationed there. Bill Wynne was more used to the farmland and industrial landscape of Ohio where you could see for miles around. Here, the jungle was a hiding place for predators of all kinds, including the enemy who were more wise to the terrain and therefore assumed to always be one step ahead.

This was to be Smoky's playground. And her whole body shook with excitement just looking at it. A strange whimpering cry escaped from her body: a sound that was loud enough to come from a much larger animal. Bill's first impression was that she liked what she saw and, although she was still a little limp and weak from her traumas, Bill could feel her tiny feet digging into his side as if she wanted to scramble out of his grasp and have a run around her new home. But first there was something Bill had to do.

Bill's tent mate was Ed Downey who was definitely not going to welcome the tiny new resident. There was only one way to handle this and that was to deal with it there and then, head on. With Smoky still cradled in his arms, Bill looked at Ed and declared, short and sweet and low, 'She stays!' It seemed odd to Bill that Downey, the man who had saved Smoky from almost certain death in the jungle, so vehemently resented her presence in the tent. But perhaps it explains why, when he knew how much Bill wanted a dog, that he didn't present him with his find instead of dropping her at the motor pool. But, a combination of luck, love and loyalty have a habit of winning through in the end; no matter how many obstacles are thrown in their path they rise up, like a resilient garden weed determined to make their presence felt no matter what. In this case, the dog and the man met anyway and the match was made. It was love at first sight and there was no turning back.

Smoky fell in love with something at first sight too – Bill's cot. Once out of his arms she scampered towards it and then dived onto the drab olive cover folded at the bottom. She circled her chosen spot a couple of times and then settled down for a nap. Bill watched her every move. Her dreadful make-do haircut was severe and the crudely cropped tufts of hair all over her body made her look as if she had been the victim of some terrible attack. But her coat fascinated Bill and he tried to imagine how it would have looked before Dare's impromptu cut. He could see why Dare had called her Smokums as the colour of her coat was a gingery brown with smoky tips and he imagined that when it all grew back the hair would be fairly long and flowing. Right now, the lack of hair meant her tiny fine-boned legs were on display and her delicate face and features could be seen clearly – at least that would help Bill give her a check-over when she woke. For now he wanted to let her sleep in comfort and peace. It would give him time to gather a few things together for his role as dog owner – one of the first bits of kit he was going to need for her in this humid environment, was a bath. Bill reached for his helmet – if it was good enough to act as his shaving basin then it was good enough to double-up as a dog bath.

As Smoky lay dozing on his cot, Bill took a moment to come to terms with his new responsibility. He had realized, within seconds of having her in his arms, that although she was the size of a lap dog she was not going to be content sitting on anyone's lap all day, or lying on their bed. He did not know what breed she was but he could see that she was something special. She was tiny, and he could see there was a canine elegance and grace about her. But those were not the qualities that were going to help her now. More important to her in the jungle was her unstinting spirit. Bill could see she had an element of mischief in her make-up. He had witnessed too her sheer determination and he felt relieved because these were the qualities that were going to be the most valuable in her day-to-day survival alongside soldiers in a war zone.

Bill and Smoky were now players together in the war in the Pacific. They were part of a combined military force that was fighting the Japanese Imperial Army on land, at sea, and in the air. To win this battle it was going to need soldiers, sailors and airmen with not only the hardware to cripple the enemy but the emotional and psychological strength to take them through the bullets and the bombs and back home safe.

When Smoky was adopted by Private First Class Bill Wynne it was March 1944 and the United States of America had been in the Second World War for just over three years. Bill was one of 150,000 US servicemen posted to the New Guinea jungle as part of the Allied mission to hold off the Japanese from reaching Australia and regain Asia. The ultimate aim was to force a Japanese surrender. This was quite a tall order considering the Japanese had clearly exercised their military might on the US on 7 December 1941 with a surprise attack on Pearl Harbor, the naval parking lot in Hawaii for some of the US Navy's finest warships. Battleships, cruisers, destroyers and more, all anchored in rows waiting to be called into the action. But they never stood a chance. Just after 7am on that Sunday morning the first wave of enemy planes bombarded the fleet destroying or severely damaging the ships where they sat. This once peaceful, paradise location had become a blazing inferno; a graveyard for several thousand tons of burning charred and twisted steel.

On 8 December, US President Franklin D. Roosevelt addressed Congress:

'Yesterday, December 7 1941 – a date which will live in infamy – the United States of America was suddenly and deliberately attacked by naval and air forces of the Empire of Japan.

… As Commander-in-Chief of the Army and Navy I have directed that all measures be taken for our defense, that always will our whole nation remember the character of the onslaught against us.

With confidence in our Armed Forces, with the unbounding determination of our people, we will gain the inevitable triumph. So help us God.

I ask that the Congress declare that since the unprovoked and dastardly attack by Japan on Sunday, December 7 1941, a state of war has existed between the United States and the Japanese Empire.'

The cream of the US fleet was crippled. Battleship row decimated. On 7 December, Japan also launched an attack against Malaya and then Hong Kong. They also entered Guam and the Philippine Islands. They attacked Wake Island and, the following morning, Midway Island.

Meanwhile, the war in Europe was still raging. Hitler's Luftwaffe was doing its worst against the city of London, the nightly bombing raids causing mass destruction to people's homes in an attempt to break the spirit of the British people. To those engaged in the war in Europe, the conflict in the Pacific must have seemed light years away. The US Navy and the 5th Air Force had destroyed Japanese landing forces destined for Australia in the Coral Sea Battle in June 1942 and would force the point again a little while later in the Battle of Midway. And to continue to keep the enemy at bay it was going to need a huge injection of troops. It was thought this could only be achieved once the war in Europe was over. The Allied Forces and the political machine behind them fought to keep the Japanese threat at a distance for as long as they could – preferably until Hitler had been defeated, all occupied territory liberated and British shores secured. In March 1943, young GIs like Bill Wynne were facing two years of jungle warfare in a place very far from home.

When Bill Wynne read the headlines declaring the attack on Pearl Harbor he was home in Cleveland, Ohio.

He was nineteen years old and a graduate of West Technical High School, the second largest public school in the country. His passion for football had been satisfied with a spell in the first team but torn ligaments in his right knee saw off any chance of a continued performance. On an academic front, West Tech offered a wide variety of courses to attract the more practically minded student and that suited Bill. Everything was geared to turn out work fodder for local industries and the vast acreage of greenhouses. Alongside courses for prospective electricians, carpenters, pattern makers and printers, there was an outstanding course in horticulture, which interested Bill, as did photography and art which he studied for a year.

Bill was still a student when he met the love of his life, Margie Roberts. His family moved into her street, just a few doors down from her house. The attraction was mutual and instant and for Bill, who had moved house ten times before reaching the age of seventeen, it was the best move of all. He still believes it was meant to be. It was Margie who bought Bill his first dog, Toby, who was only six weeks old when he was presented as a twentieth birthday gift on 29 March 1942. A German Shepherd and Doberman cross, Toby became Bill's reason to attend his first dog training class. The Cleveland All Breeds Training School was Bill's introduction to formal dog training classes. The classes were organized with the blessing of the American Kennel Club and incorporated a great many of the techniques being used to train dogs attached to the Armed Forces as patrol and guard dogs. The Services would require dogs that could display the ultimate in discipline and control and nothing less. The training was adapted to suit the average dog owner and their pet but the ten week programme was rigid and many owners' expectations were high. The classes proved very popular and owners came from miles around to attend. Although Bill did not know this at the time, the training was going to be more relevant in the future than in the present.

Having Toby in his life was a huge step forward for Bill, perhaps more than Margie realized at the time. Bill wasn't new to dog ownership but it was a relationship that had brought with it the ultimate in pleasure of partnership and the pain of loss. Bill's childhood was punctuated with periods of sadness but somehow there was always a dog to be his companion and to lead him to laughter and happiness.

Bill's mother and father separated in 1925 when Bill was six years old. His mother had to take a full-time job which was relatively well paid for a woman but childcare was impossible to secure when she needed it. Reluctantly, she had to reach a temporary compromise that would enable her to continue to support her family and that was to send Bill and his younger brother, Jim, to the nearby

Parmadale Orphanage while their sister Mary went to live with her grandmother in Scranton. Bill would be at the orphanage for two years.

At Parmadale, Bill met the first dog in his life, Rags, a friendly Airedale who loved all the children and they loved him. Rags loved to run and play with them and never seemed to be exhausted by their games. But one day, one of the older and more difficult children took their frustration out on the dog by pouring acid over his body. Horrified, the other children could only look on as the dog ran from his tormentor. Rags' cries have echoed in Bill's head ever since.

The Parmadale days were not unhappy ones but going home was the best of times and one thing that made it all the happier was Skippy. Bill was five when he said good-bye to the orphanage and settled back home and one of his first memories of coming home was seeing Skippy tied to the kitchen door handle. The large white Collie dog had proven early on that he loved to run but didn't always come back. If he escaped it took the entire street to chase him, corner him and take him home. His barking often annoyed the neighbours too but one night, just as the next door neighbours were about to get up and complain to Mrs Wynne, they realized their house was on fire. Skippy was not being a nuisance – he was saving their lives. This dog was the first to show Bill that when it comes to dogs, what you see is not always the sum total of what you get. Skippy was not a nuisance dog at all, he was a local hero.

Although Bill never owned the Great Dane called Big Boy, he was as close as you can get to your best friend's dog. George Harsa was a friendly boy and his dog matched his character perfectly. Wherever Big Boy went, George was bound to follow, and Bill too. They were friends from their first meeting. Walking and playing in West 119th Street with the huge mutt bounding along beside them, the boys were happy as the day was long. At eight years old, no one should have a care in the world and this was so true of George and Bill. In the evenings, George would entertain the neighbourhood children with his banjo playing and Big Boy would sit alongside him, his most faithful fan. It was a relationship that Bill longed for for himself. The days at Parmadale were mostly happy but the discipline was harsh, even for children of only three years old. The sting of the half-inch wooden stick that often slapped down on his hand was something he would not forget. When Queenie wandered into his life, their relationship seemed meant to be. Bill was out playing and Queenie, whose breed was somewhat mixed to say the least, came to see what he was all about. She was quiet and friendly and interested in everything he had to tell her. She was so engrossed that she followed Bill home and his mother let her stay. Like all the dogs that found refuge in the Wynne household,

Queenie was absorbed into the family's life. She was a friend to all but it was Bill she would follow to the end of the earth. Queenie settled so well into the neighbourhood that she was able to present her family with a litter of pups. All adorable and all possessing Queenie's calm and loving temperament, the pups were popular and had plenty of visitors. The whole neighbourhood grieved when Queenie was killed in a road traffic accident. She had made quite an impact, especially on the children.

It was lucky for Bill's mother that one of the litter, Pal, was still around to comfort her young son. Pal was more of a breed mix than his mother but every inch of his stocky, brindle body said that he was Bill's protector. There was certainly a little Chow Chow and some Bull Terrier in the mix and a good deal more besides to make up his muscular body. Pal loved everyone and everyone loved Pal. He didn't like other dogs very much but every child in town felt he was their pet and Bill was happy to share him. Bill was always teaching Pal new tricks such as riding downhill on a sled and then pulling the pile of sleds back to the top of the hill. He could jump in the air and take a hat off someone's head and hand the hat back to them. Bill loved showing off Pal's tricks.

Bill and Pal were a real partnership and looked after each other. Every time they came close to the busy road that ran behind Wynne's house, Bill would stop and say, 'Up!' and Pal would jump into his arms and be carried safely over the road. The same would happen if Bill saw a rival dog coming towards them. But Pal's best trick of all was working out how to get to Bill's school. No one had shown him the route, he just seemed to find it one day and there he was waiting outside the school gate at home time. After that, he did the same thing everyday at 3.30 p.m. and walked Bill home. Then one day, after about a year, he wasn't there. Bill searched high and low for any trace of his dog. The neighbourhood turned out to help but he was no where to be found. Pal never came home again. He was gone and it broke Bill's heart.

So, when Toby came into Bill's life some years later, the relationship had a bittersweet beginning. Having Toby brought back all the memories of Pal, the dog that gave him so much joy in his childhood, a joy that was as real and tangible as the hardships he had experienced during the Depression of the 1930s. The Depression had a catastrophic effect on Bill's family and its fortunes. Of course they weren't alone in that. The Wall Street Crash put an end to Bill's mother's well-paid job and meant she had to move her family around in order to chase work and an affordable rent. It was why they moved house so often, finally settling when Bill was seventeen.

At that point, life changed for the better in so many ways. Turning from a boy who showed little interest in schoolbooks, Bill became a dedicated and successful student. He met his sweetheart, Margie, and then Toby, the dog came pattering along. Toby was going to receive all the attention that Bill missed giving to his beloved Pal; the dog he vowed would be his last. There was a new challenge too: his desire to marry and set up home with Margie which meant making money became the focus of each day. Working in the local foundry was hard and heavy work but Bill was able to work two shifts a day to support the war effort and his own personal effort to save money. And Toby? He accompanied Bill to work and enjoyed long naps on the warm brick floor. Pressure was building on the foundry to step up production. The demand for steel to feed the manufacture of fighter planes, ships and munitions was heightening to the point where the foundry's furnaces were ablaze twenty-four hours a day. Bill could have worked around the clock but the arrival of his draft papers cut that plan short. His country needed him and Bill answered that call.

Bill was assigned to the 5th Fighter Command of the 5th Air Force at Port Moresby in New Guinea. His interest and qualification in photography had made him a perfect recruit for air reconnaissance duties and, after completing a laboratory technician course, he qualified as an aerial photographer. In any other time and under any other circumstances the balmy breeze that rippled around them would have been a luxury to enjoy and relax in but not this location. There was always the threat of a red alert – the warning to take cover as enemy bombers attacked the airfield. The 'ack-ack' of the anti-aircraft guns continued throughout the night. For a while, Bill and Ed Downey helped out with general duties on the camp but Ed was frustrated and convinced the commanding officers had forgotten they had two aerial photographers and felt their skills were not being utilized. Ed was not afraid to make a fuss and his film-star looks and presence made him a force to be reckoned with. An immediate transfer to 5212th Photographic Wing meant a posting to Nadzab to take up a position as an aerial photographer.

Bill and Ed were there as General David W. Hutchinson's personal photographers but Photo Hutch, as he was nicknamed, had crashed his B17 while on a mission on Boxing Day of 1943, just before the two photographers arrived. After an awkward start, they were assigned to the photographic laboratory. Their boss, Captain Powell had developed an aerial camera mount for low-level bombing photography and this development was made at a crucial time for the Allies. As a member of the 26th Photo Reconnaissance Squadron, Bill was part of an elite force whose activities were vital to the success of the war in the Pacific. There was a saying that the side with the best aerial reconnaissance team was the one that would win the war. Bill and Smoky were a part of the best.

While Bill was working twelve-hour shifts in the photo lab, Smoky would accompany him and entertain the other technicians just by being with them. Sitting on one of the trays used for passing wet images outside for washing in the daylight, Smoky would be passed between the men. And she was acquiring a wide range of tricks to show off. When he wasn't at work, Bill would spend his time teaching Smoky something new. The little dog was a good pupil and picked up tricks very quickly and, more than that, she was eager to please. Her favourite party trick was playing dead: Bill would point his finger at her and shout, 'Bang!' This was Smoky's signal to fall onto her side. From that point she would remain limp and still, and no matter how many times Bill prodded her, swung her round or tried to wake her she remained totally lifeless. The audience loved it. Then, with one word from Bill – 'OK' – she sprung to her feet and dashed to her master for some well-deserved praise. Smoky's antics helped fill the long and lonely hours spent waiting for news of the Japanese invasion.

Formed in 1943, the 26th Photo Recon Squadron was vital to the war effort and its planes were constantly on or near the front line throughout the war. The planes were F-5s, stripped down, customized versions of the P-38 Lockhead Lightening one-seater fighters. They had to be light and manoeuvrable so they could get in fast, get the shots and get out again so the armoured protection on the fuselage and the guns were removed. All the time the planes would be drawing enemy fire, but were unable to fire back. It was the only way to find out where enemy troops were positioned along with their hardware and ammunition. The images the recon teams captured could prove invaluable evidence of enemy activity to share with the Army, Navy and Air Force. Each flight entailed risking life and limb with only a camera for protection.

Hollandia, in Dutch New Guinea, was approximately 450 miles from Nadzab and had three aerodromes which harboured the remainder of Japanese air strength in that area. It was surrounded by a range of 6,000-foot high mountains which would make any approach more problematic. But due south, in We Wak, there was a reported force of around 200,000 Japanese troops fresh from combat in China. The strategy was to starve them out by cutting off supplies from the outside world. Air reconnaissance revealed there were 350 enemy planes: the 5th Air Force wiped them out in three days.

Only one thing could stop a recon team in its tracks were the big, black tropical storms which swept the area. Cruel and destructive, the storms cancelled out the daylight making flying dangerous and photography impossible. On Black Sunday, 1944, a sudden storm turned day into night in seconds. Out of 200 B-2s, four B-25s and A-20 bombers, eighteen per cent were lost in the air and on the ground. 5th Air Force alone lost thirty-seven. Those in the air either lost sight of the mountains or ran out of fuel.

The storms were an unpredictable force of nature and the bane of the recon team. Smoky was not keen on them either. Bill soon learned that his dog could predict a storm several hours before it hit. Smoky would go very quiet and sniff the air before she began to whimper and then head for Bill's cot. She knew the storms were bad news and did her best to warn the men. It was just another way she paid Bill back for taking her into his care.

Of course, Bill and his friends were always looking out for Smoky too. One of the big health threats in the jungle was Scrub Typhus. Nine out of ten sufferers died and Smoky, being the perfect host for the ticks that carried the disease was in a vulnerable position. It was decided she would have a daily bath in Bill's helmet to help keep her tick-free, and Smoky loved it. The relief of the tepid wash was a joy to her and she seemed to smile as Bill swished the water over her body. Carefully, Bill would lift her out of the make-shift bathtub and pat her dry, feeling for the telltale lump of the insects on her body. Bill's heart was in his throat each time he started to examine her. He knew that if she was sick there would be no veterinary help available.

Smoky had mastered the basics of Bill's recall training: when he called her she returned immediately so he knew it was safe to let her run free in the jungle – she would always come back. And it was wonderful to watch her chase the birds and the giant exotic butterflies as she looked so happy and free. In those special moments, watching Smoky, it was as if the war was non-existent and it was a normal day in the sunshine, a day spent relaxing with friends, not a care in the world. A sudden burst of gunfire would usually bring everyone back to their senses and the moment of normality would pass as quickly as it had been conjured up. There were pressing realities that had to be faced up to.

The scare of the Scrub Typhus made Bill and his friends face the fact that Smoky's life was potentially in danger. They decided that Smoky had to be confined to barracks, only venturing as far as the tether tied to Bill's bed would allow. And there were other concerns in the jungle too: pythons. A python would have found Smoky a tasty bite-size meal and Bill was well aware of that danger. There was also the constant worry of her being kidnapped by someone else. She liked to chase the native humpbacked hens and that's probably how she ran into one of the local villages where the children discovered that she was far more intelligent than the average camp dog. Bill was used to losing sight of her for short periods of time but that day he was terrified she had gone forever. Unable to speak the native language of Papua New Guinea and aware that some of the tribes were cannibals,

Bill had to face his fears and ask a group of local people if they had seen his dog. At first, the language barrier looked as though it would stifle his enquiries but then his short impersonation of Smoky barking, raising a paw and standing on her hind legs was enough to communicate with the man who beckoned Bill to follow him. Leaving the dusty path, Bill followed full of eagerness to see Smoky again but all the time knowing he had no idea what he was going to see. When he stepped into the clearing, he could hear Smoky barking and his heart leapt in anguish until he recognized it was her happy bark. The village children were sitting around her and Smoky was running through her repertoire of tricks for them. The joy on their little faces was clear for all to see. The more laughter Smoky generated, the more she wanted to entertain. Bill felt almost guilty for depriving her of her enthusiastic audience. But Smoky didn't mind. One look at Bill and she saw home and everything was good again. The children all kissed her goodbye and Bill and Smoky waved as they disappeared back through the jungle and found the pathway onto the main track. It was a surreal moment but another little miracle in the centre of the hostilities. A moment that, in any other time and circumstance, would have been ordinary. But not here and not now.

The more Smoky established herself in the camp, the higher her profile became and there were always jealous eyes on her. She was small and cute. She was friendly and talented. And, although there were other canine mascots adopted by the soldiers, Smoky stood out from the crowd. It seemed that keeping her close to him was the only way Bill could be sure she would remain safe. The risk of losing her was too great to take.

Smoky's tricks became part of the daily entertainment in the camp, especially in the print room where Bill worked. Their impromptu shows were a welcome distraction from the pressure of the job and the fear that resulted from the random snippets of news they received about the status of the Japanese invasion and the war beyond their far-away section of the Pacific. Of course, news of Smoky's talents spread beyond the confines of the 26th Camp and it didn't take long for *Yank Down Under* magazine to track man and dog down. The magazine had launched a mascot competition and was keen for Bill to enter Smoky even though the squadron had already entered its existing mascot, a monkey called Colonel Turbo. At first, Bill was reluctant to take up the challenge. He could think of all the reasons why Smoky should not be entered into the competition but he was underestimating the enthusiasm of the dog's fan base. Bill had to concede due to public demand and once he had done that he wanted the image they sent to the magazine to be perfect. Ideas fluttered into his head until his mind was buzzing with winning shots of Smoky as a military mascot. First he grabbed his helmet and put it on the ground. He knew Smoky would jump right in as she would be expecting a bath, and she loved baths. Bill took the shots himself and was very pleased with the results – Smoky looked so happy to be there and she adored being the centre of attention. But for the next idea, Bill was going to need some help.

The idea was to photograph Smoky descending by parachute. A creative idea, but with one problem: they needed a parachute, or at least a part of one to make the shot believable. Everyone was keen for Smoky to win the competition and besides, it made a pleasant diversion from the other off-duty pastimes. Within no time at all a 'find Smoky a parachute' project team had formed with Bill at its helm. The first item called in was the pilot's parachute which was quickly adapted to Smoky's size and then a collection of belts were added to create a harness. Bill then took a little time out with Smoky to practise the swinging to-and-fro movements so she wouldn't be spooked later on. In the meantime, it was agreed that the drop needed to be about thirty feet from a tree with Bill and a buddy ready to catch the dog in a GI blanket at the bottom. Branches were sawn off a nearby tree to accommodate the parachuting dog and in no time at all, Smoky was in Bill's safe hands in the tree. The plan worked perfectly and the men knew they had the shots they wanted. Smoky seemed so happy as a parachute dog that they couldn't resist doing it a few more times, just for fun.

What the men hadn't noticed was the slight breeze that had been so helpful up until now was growing stronger and with Smoky set for her final drop, the wind caught the chute, which collapsed and then swept the tiny 'para' off course. Free falling at speed, Smoky yelped in panic. She tried several times to correct herself and managed to land on her feet but then bounced twice leaving her on her back. Bill dashed to where Smoky was lying. He saw her little body lying limp and helpless on the ground and thought the worst. *Why did I do that? Why did I carry on with the jumps when I had the shot I needed?* Bill chastised himself for getting carried away with the whole parachuting dog idea. He knew he would never forgive himself if anything had happened to Smoky because of his sheer stupidity. Maybe it was a slight concussion? Maybe she just wanted to teach him a lesson in taking better care of her? Whatever it was, the moments (that seemed like hours to Bill) passed and finally the fear-ridden GI could feel Smoky's body stir in his hands. She looked up at him, as much to say: 'Hey you. What did you think you were playing at, buddy? No more games like that one, please.' Bill heard every word and guilt swept over him. He vowed, there and then, not to abuse her trust in him again. She did everything he asked of her, even jumped out of a tree. But that was to be the last time.

Of course, Smoky was perfectly capable of getting herself into scrapes singlehanded. Watching a game of softball has to be one of the safest activities no matter where you are, but maybe not if you are mistaken for the ball! Everything was fine while Smoky sat on Bill's lap watching the game but suddenly she decided to join in the action on the field. Reaching third base, she caught the attention of the player who mistook her for the ball and scooped her up. He was all ready to throw to second base when he realized what was in his hand. Smoky had made a fantastic run but it was all about to end horribly. Bill's frantic shouting and the realization of the players saved Smoky from a dash to the ground. It was a lesson to her to sit quietly next time.

Sitting in the middle of a war zone, it's easy to imagine how you might be hurt or injured but the jungle brings its own hidden dangers and mosquitoes are always a major problem in the Tropics. The drug Atrabine was part of the soldier's protection against malaria and it was easy to spot anyone who was on a regular dosage due to the yellow tinge to their skin. When Bill fell ill with dengue fever, his only chance of recovery was a transfer to the 3rd Field Hospital in Nadzab. All front-line combat troops were treated here and Bill found himself surrounded by battle-weary servicemen. Bill's war, so far, had only been touched by one aspect of the conflict and the invaluable part his reconnaissance squadron were playing; here in the hospital all victims of this particular theatre of war were assembled under one roof. Bill was in no state to judge where he was or what was going on but he knew that Smoky would be safe with his friend, Frank Petnilak, and that was all that mattered.

After three days in hospital, Bill was allowed one visitor and it was someone he hadn't expected to see at his bedside for some time: Smoky. She was not only allowed on the ward, but she was also allowed to sleep on Bill's bed and it was agreed she could stay as long as necessary to help with his recovery. But Smoky was not the only delivery that day. With her came a copy of the latest issue of *Yank Down Under* announcing Smoky as Champion Mascot of the SWPA (South West Pacific Area). Everyone was hugely excited and Bill was so proud of his little dog. Bill's image of her in his GI helmet had won her the competition. She was the heroine of the hospital.

The Red Cross nurses were so taken with Smoky that they asked Bill if he would allow them to take her to visit other patients. Bill was delighted. He still remembers the look on the faces of the wounded when Smoky appeared on the ward: 'It was as if the men had seen a vision. Perhaps because it was something so unexpected that they could not believe it: a look of half surprise and sheer delight. I never forgot the effect Smoky had on those men fresh from conflict. The picture stayed with me way beyond the war years. It was a little miracle.' Even the most battle-worn combat soldier found a smile for the little dog with the big personality.

During her stay, the nurses would often borrow Smoky and take her to see some of the wounded being brought in from Biak and Wakde Islands. Some had been wounded in mortar bomb attacks and were desperately ill but the sight of the little dog and her cheerful face lifted their spirits in a way medication never could.

As Bill waited for the doctors to agree his discharge from hospital, he heard that his squadron was preparing to leave for action in Hollandia. There was also some news on Smoky's identity: not how she came to be in the jungle in the first place but a definitive report on her breed. Bill took the copy of *National Geographic* that a colleague handed to him and read with interest a feature called: *Dogs in Toyland*. One of the pictures showed a dog that was the image of Smoky and it was captioned: 'Yorkshire Terrier'. There it was in black and white. Bill avidly read the article and it was clear that his dog was an excellent example of the breed. He always knew she had breeding and class but this just proved it to everyone. Smoky was a Yorkie. But how a dog of such incredible breeding made it to New Guinea still remained a mystery.

Bill had survived dengue fever, many others had not and as far as he was concerned, that was another miracle bestowed on him. He felt well enough to return to active service but the medics were not convinced and decided his recovery should be completed away from the war zone. So his reunion with Smoky coincided with being given a fifteen-day leave pass to Brisbane, Australia. Always fearful that Smoky would be confiscated by the authorities if she was discovered, Bill was careful to hide her and the hiding place this time was a musette bag, a small canvas kit bag with straps to fasten it. Bill taught her to stay still and quiet and she knew to do this as soon as he put her inside it. It was now August 1944 and hiding in the bag was a routine she was to perfect. Hitching a ride in a C-47 (a Gooney Bird) to Port Moresby was easy except the plane (capable of carrying 5,000 pounds cargo weight) was so over the limit that Bill and Smoky had to sit in with the pilot to redistribute some weight! The flight on to Townsville, near Brisbane, was uneventful but the temperature in the cockpit gave them an idea of how cold it was going to be on the ground. When they landed and were taken to their billet, Bill took one look at Smoky's shivering body and asked for six blankets. He could tell they were going to need them. They were no longer in the Tropics and, although the heat was often stifling there, it was what they were used to. When they arrived, Smoky was shivering violently. Although they were missing the heat, there were a few things they could enjoy for the first time in eight months: fresh meat, for one and fresh milk for another.

The cold was something Smoky was really not used to at all. She had been living in the heat of the jungle for most of her life … maybe all of her life. The blankets were fine for her naps and overnight but Smoky was cold all the time. Bill had to find her a coat. A hobby shop did not seem the obvious choice for someone looking for a dog's coat but, as it happened, a green wool and felt cover for a card table provided the ideal solution. It had a beaded edge and was large enough to be fashioned into a warm coat that could also be used to display Smoky's growing collection of campaign badges. One of the Red Cross volunteers offered her services as Smoky's seamstress and in no time at all she had made the coat and added the decorations that Bill provided: the 5th Air Force patch, the dog's corporal's stripes, the US insignia, a small brass propeller button (sewn onto all enlisted men's blousons), the 26th Recon emblem, two 'six month overseas' bars, the Asian Pacific Ribbon and perhaps most precious of all, the Good Conduct Ribbon. The coat was complete and Smoky couldn't wait to snuggle into its deep warmth. Bill was delighted with the result and the love and dedication that had gone into making it so special for his little dog. All this and eggs and steak for breakfast. What more could a little dog ask?

For this little dog, there was one thing she loved more than her new coat and that was an audience to entertain. Wherever Smoky went, the Red Cross nurses were quick to find Bill and ask if his dog could go along to visit the patients. Bill was always happy to oblige as he knew the magic of having the dog around to fuss and talk to and there would always be a few tricks to share with everyone. The 109th Fleet Naval hospital was the venue for their first show. The audience was made up of sailors and Marines who had been transferred to Australia because the climate was more conducive to healing their wounds. In the Tropics this was a long and unpredictable process that many did not survive. Looking at the men sitting in front of him, Bill recognized the misery of hospitalization etched on their faces. Surly nothing could break the cycle of fear and frustration these men were facing every day? Nothing, that is, until Smoky made her grand entrance. Once again just the presence of the little dog lit up the room and the faces of the people waiting to see her. Without any hesitation, Bill signalled to Smoky to 'play dead' and the show began. Everyone in all eight wards of the hospital enjoyed the show and every one of Smoky's tricks but it was the chance to stroke and fuss her at the end that really gave the men a boost.

She followed this performance with a visit to the US 42nd General Army Hospital in Brisbane where she put on a show in twelve of the wards. Some of the patients followed her from ward to ward so they could see the show and meet Smoky several times over. She was a smash hit in every hospital and always followed the show-biz rule of leaving her audience wanting more.

As Bill's recovery leave drew to an end, preparations were made to return him to his squadron. The 26th Photo Recon Squadron was destined for service on Biak Island and for Bill the fear was not of battle but whether Smoky would be allowed to go with him. There were rumours that the dreaded Scrub Typhus was causing devastation on the island but other dogs were there and so it had to be worth taking the chance with Smoky even if she had to be smuggled there. Biak Island was a coral battleground located just four degrees south of the Equator. The white coral landscape stretched for twenty-five miles and offered a bare and hostile environment to the US troops stationed there. The invading Japanese Army had inhabited the many caves that could be found all over the island but rumour had it that 5,000 of their soldiers were still holding ground all over Biak.

When 26th Photo Recon arrived on Biak, the US infantry patrol based there for the clean-up operation put a call out for volunteers. A first sergeant stepped forward for the experience with the idea that he would see what was required of these volunteers before others put their names down. After three days, he returned with first-hand reports of face-to-face encounters with enemy soldiers. He confirmed to the commanding officer,

Captain McCullough, that to volunteer for this clean-up mission meant being prepared for combat. The soldier had six notches on his M1 Garand service rifle to prove that he had encountered the enemy and despatched them accordingly in the intensity of jungle warfare. It was clear to the captain that anyone who followed from the 26th would, like any other infantryman, be facing the same horror and he decided there would be no more volunteers from his squadron as they were too vital to lose. Every air recon crew risked their lives on every flight but the images they captured of the enemy's position saved many thousands of lives. There were no more volunteer requests and the photo lab was soon pressed to working twenty-four-hour shifts developing thousands of negatives and tens of thousands of prints for distribution to the Allied Forces on land, in the air and at sea. The dedication of Bill's team was recognized with its first Presidential Unit Citation for outstanding coverage of the Philippine Islands from 18–20 September 1944. At that time there were sixty-five men in the lab turning out 650,000 prints which were delivered to the 6th Army, the Air Corps, the Navy and the Australian Forces. Through these images the war in the Pacific was co-ordinated and fought.

The weather always controlled the activities of the recon squadrons. When the storms set in, the planes could be grounded for days even weeks leaving the men anxious and in need of something to distract them from reality. This is where Smoky came into her own. She loved to swim with Bill and it was the perfect way to cool down in temperatures reaching 54°C inside their tent. She was too small to dive into the ocean with everyone else but a four-foot-deep bomb crater proved to be the perfect paddling pool for little Smoky. She loved having her own private pool on the beach, not to mention all the attention she attracted from her admirers who loved to see her enjoy herself. But, the salt water was not kind to her coat which was, at long last, starting to grow out of the GI crop that she had when Bill first met her. She was now looking more like the Yorkie pictured in the *National Geographic* magazine except the ocean salt was setting hard on each strand making it course and matted. But this was nothing Bill couldn't solve with a daily fresh-water bath: half a helmet full for the bath and half for the rinse. Perfect.

It was Smoky's attitude to life in a war zone that was so important to the men. It didn't seem to matter how hot it was and how fiercely the sun reflected off the white coral surroundings or how bad-tempered people became due to the white heat or the drowning rain or sheer fear of what could happen next, Smoky was always happy. It was as if she refused to let any of the harshness get her down. She was happy to find shelter under Bill's cot or enjoy a cooling bath. If she had the energy she would chase birds

or, if she felt like really making mischief, she could see if
the monkey, Colonel Turbo, was up for a fight. Colonel
Turbo was the mascot of 25th Photo Recon Squadron
and he had a reputation for being a nasty piece of work.
The pilot who had bought the rhesus monkey from a zoo
in New Mexico when the men were on manoeuvres, had
died when his plane crashed so the squadron decided to
keep Turbo as their mascot in memory of the lost pilot. It
was a lovely idea and an admirable act of respect but it
was something they would grow to regret as Turbo settled
into his destructive and aggressive ways. If he wasn't
running rampage in the tents stealing food and eating
cigarettes he was most likely biting the hand that fed him.
And almost every man in the squadron had the marks to
prove it.

When Smoky first met Turbo, the 26th Recon was
warned that the monkey would mangle the dog – Turbo
had a track record for doing that with dogs. Everyone
watched with interest. Bill knew that Turbo was tethered
on a length of rope so he set Smoky down where the
monkey's leash was at full stretch. After a moment or two
of sniffing each other from a distance Turbo suddenly
flew at Smoky sinking his teeth into her nose. Yelping
with pain and shock Smoky turned from her aggressor
and then suddenly turned back and flew at him scratching his nose. Nothing and no one had ever done that to
him before and Turbo scampered up his favourite tree to

lick his wounds. He sat there for a few moments just touching his nose and then checking his paw for blood before dashing back down to run at Smoky. Turning on him again, she sent the confused monkey back to his tree. He refused to come down. No dog had ever threatened him or hurt him as Smoky had done and it was the start of a love/hate relationship that was to last until Turbo carried out his final act of destruction. It was hoped that he would die of natural causes as he was something of a mascot hero in the Pacific and his squadron was always faithful to him.

Smoky always thought it was good sport to chase and chastise Turbo, knowing he was on the end of a rope. But his temper grew worse and the tidal wave of destruction he created when he managed to free himself from the rope began to annoy more people. One day, a shot was fired close to the camp and after that Turbo disappeared. It was a sad end to the career of an animal that had seen so much active service.

Smoky's antics with Colonel Turbo were always entertaining but one of the major distractions from the work of war were Smoky's training sessions. Bill had already taught her a handful of tricks but there were many more he wanted her to perform for this captive audience. Walking a tightrope, blindfolded, was the next on the list and for that he needed the help of some of his colleagues.

In no time at all, a platform for the wires had been constructed and two aircraft control cables stretched between the pipes. The whole structure was then secured into the coral for safety. Bill and Smoky repeated the routine on the rope over and over again and all the time Smoky gained confidence until she had enough trust in Bill to do the walk blindfolded with only his voice to guide her. Once that was perfected, Bill set his sights on seeing Smoky walk on a barrel. Finding the barrel was the easy part as the chemicals used in the photo lab were shipped in fifty-five gallon barrels so all Bill had to do was have one cut down in size and then have it painted circus style. Bill knew this was a complex trick but he also knew that Smoky was intelligent and would master it. Perhaps he was expecting too much too soon from her. Perhaps it was the 37°C heat that was getting to her – she kept falling on her side and she looked so exhausted. Bill decided to give her a rest and he set Smoky down on his cot to sleep. A little while later, he noticed something small and black lying next to Smoky. He couldn't quite make it out but as he drew closer to the blob on the bed he could see that it was moving. It was a puppy. Smoky's puppy and he didn't even know she was pregnant. Bill was in shock. It was great news but so unexpected. He recalled someone saying that Smoky had found a boyfriend during the time Bill was making his way back from hospital in Nadzab. He had dismissed the idea as a joke but obviously it was true. The likely father was Duke, another Terrier. This one belonged to Bill's friend, John Hembury, and there was sure to be lots of interest from his camp too. Bill decided to call the puppy Topper and Smoky proved to be a good and attentive mother. The men celebrated the arrival of Smoky's puppy in style, thanks to a little help of a delivery by a B-25 Mitchell bomber (a Fat Cat). The B-25s were often used to test flying times and, in their stripped down form (with no armour plating and no weapons), they were filled with cargo such as cases of alcohol, fresh fruit and meat and all the other items it was impossible to acquire on Biak. Sometimes the plane was so full of goodies that the bomb doors would not close! It was a good job the latest drop was a generous one as people came from miles around to see the new arrival. They wondered how a dog that was only four pounds in weight herself could produce a pup. Everyone was happy to toast the youngster's arrival with a class of homemade Cola made from Coke syrup, water and compressed aircraft oxygen tank. It was improvised and inspired. Everyone loved it and Topper was welcomed into the 26th Photo Squadron in style many times over. Smoky joined in each toast with an enthusiastic bark.

On 16 September 1944, Bill was informed that his flying status had been confirmed. As a graduate of aerial photo school, he was eligible for combat duty and this provided him with the opportunity to leave the photo lab and earn the required 300 combat hours (time spent 'where enemy fire is probable and expected'). A young lieutenant from 3rd Emergency Rescue Squadron (3 ERS) needed a photographer to accompany him on a mission to find a pilot missing in action behind enemy lines. An aerial search was the best chance they had of pinpointing his location which would greatly assist the infantry in a rescue mission. Bill prepared himself for the flight by donning his summer flying overalls then his shoulder holster containing a .45-calibre automatic pistol a clip of bullets, some birdshot and a Bowie knife. In Bill's opinion, the plane, a Stinson L-5 Sentinal, seemed too small for the task but once in the air Bill could see how it responded immediately to the pilot's demands. At an altitude of 800 feet they had a clear view over the white coral landscape with its ridges and scrub growth right down to the flatter area where, at just 50 feet from the ground, the pilot could point out a crop of foxholes that had until the day before been occupied by Japanese soldiers. They had been cleared with grenades. Flying low and slow they picked up a mound with a crater in the centre and at the bottom an Allison engine. Debris was scattered all around. No one would have survived such an impact. Bill captured the scene on film before the pilot headed towards the ocean and there, in shallow water, was a Zero fighter plane lying on the ocean bed in perfect condition.

There was no sign of the pilot although it was possible he had survived the descent. It was time to head back having clocked up thirty-five minutes combat time.

When back with the 26th, Bill recounted the details of the flight as he gave Smoky some much demanded attention. They were not often apart but it was going to be that way for some time now while Bill was in the air. But a random comment from one of the guys had Bill thinking differently: 'Hey, Wynne, if you get knocked off, I can have Smoky, can't I?' It was something Bill had not thought about, or rather had not wanted to, but knowing Smoky's fate had already been discussed in his absence made Bill sad and extremely angry. There was no way he was going to leave his dog's life in anyone else's hands. After all, he firmly believed that fate, God, or something had delivered Smoky to him and so it was his responsibility to look after her. He made the decision quickly and decisively: 'From now on she goes with me. If it happens, we go down together.' The men could see that he meant every word and said no more about it. Meanwhile, Bill took the canvas musette bag and checked the tie-down straps and the buckles and he could see how the bag's shoulder strap could be fixed around his waist and not interfere with a parachute. The plan was complete. From now on, Smoky would be his flying buddy.

Bill's next twelve missions would be in Catalina PBY-5As, otherwise known as Cats (army designation OA-10). These majestic flying boats were an integral part of 3rd Emergency Rescue Squad and flying at a maximum altitude of 13,000 feet Bill knew he could take Smoky with him as there would be no need for oxygen and he could still hide the dog in the musette bag without detection. After a hearty breakfast of bacon and eggs, Bill and Smoky were ready for their first recon flight in a Catalina. A pre-flight briefing was a chance to remind the crews of the local dangers should they crash land. A ditched air crew was a valuable commodity in the jungle. Not all the villagers were friendly to the Allies: some were pro-Japanese. Others, in Dutch New Guinea, were known to have eaten at least three US airmen.

The crew of a Catalina numbered eight people: the pilot, co-pilot, navigator, engineer mechanic, radio operator, two medics and a waist gunner. Bill, as aerial photographer, was crew member number nine. He was positioned next to the gunner in the window blister, a .50 calibre machine gun at his side. The medics doubled as gunners. Smoky was a stowaway and delivering her best performance ever, staying still and quiet until Bill was able to divulge her presence. Everyone understood why he had brought her along and it was agreed she could stay and the safest place for her bag was to hang off the top bunk. It was within Bill's reach and that was all that mattered.

It was 3 a.m. when they took off on the mission to rescue a squadron pilot missing in action. Although the plane was on a rescue and reconnaissance mission, it did not have distinctive Red Cross markings. It was marked up the same as an American war plane and was equipped to return fire. They were headed for the island of Ceram, west of the New Guinea coast and as dawn broke they entered their search area. Bill knew the lost pilot, had flown with him and that made the mission personal. He was determined to scour every inch of terrain for signs of life. But there was nothing. Suddenly and violently, the plane was pitched into a squall and everything went black. They were flying blind and being buffeted from all sides. Wrestling to keep control, the pilot climbed to 12,000 feet but the storm was still with him. The Catalina was now at the mercy of the storm and the search mission had become a matter of survival. Bill put his hand over the musette bag where Smoky was hopefully still asleep. He resisted the urge to look inside because he knew he would want to take her out and hold her but it was unsafe to do that while the plane was lurching and rolling. She was safer in the bag and while she was still and quiet, Bill was reassured. He couldn't help wondering how long she could stay quiet and calm as the storm raged around them but he hoped it would be until they entered the home stretch. For four hours the pilot, co-pilot and the navigator worked flat out to get the crew of nine men and one dog home. What had started out as a routine search had become one more victory over the violent and unpredictable weather. They were exhausted and, thankfully, as they entered the skies over Biak, the clouds lifted giving them clearance to land.

Safely back on solid ground, the men sat in the plane for a while just allowing their minds and bodies to calm. Bill unhooked the strap of the musette bag from the top bunk and put the bag over his shoulder. He felt along the bottom seam of the canvas and it was warm. He could just about feel the rise and fall of her tiny breaths; she was fine. He thanked the Good Lord and anyone else watching over them all. It was Smoky's first experience in the air and she had survived alongside Bill.

From that moment, they flew with many other crews and all of them welcomed Smoky as one of the team. It became routine that as Bill boarded the Catalina he would hang the canvas bag, with Smoky inside, on the edge of the upper bunk for the flight. On the longer flights, Bill would let her run around on the bunk for short periods just so she could stretch her legs and be reassured everything was fine. Sometimes the vibration and the loud hum of the engines was not a rhythmic comfort for her but just a loud noise that made her bark. But she was happy to be with Bill and sensing he was there made everything all right. Even when a flight turned out to be more hazardous than first thought, Bill would make sure Smoky was a happy passenger. He never took risks with his dog's safety and, at the same time, would never have compromised the pilot or any other crew member during a mission. He need not have worried about upsetting anyone, everyone was glad to have her along for the ride. Those precious moments when she was allowed out to play were special for the entire crew. They provided a short, surreal interlude from reality. Smoky had the ability to make people smile when there was very little to smile about.

One night, the Catalina with Bill and Smoky on board was due to take off at 3 a.m. to cover a bombing attack on Borneo. The bombers to follow at 5 a.m. and the fighters at 7 a.m. but bad weather halted the second and third wave leaving the ground. Consequently, the Catalina was heading for the target area alone. Not equipped for combat, the plane was now extremely vulnerable to enemy fire while still battling the weather. Bill had the aerial camera poised to take shots. It was almost impossible for the pilot to control the Catalina into a good position for Bill to take the shots he was looking for. The mantra for any recon squadron was to get in, get the shots and get out as quickly as possible but this flight was proving challenging on all fronts. The tension in the body of the plane was palpable. They sensed it was only a matter of time before enemy fighter planes would pick them up and then bring them down. Smoky was blissfully oblivious to the anxiety shared by the humans around her. It was later, when the situation was calm enough for Bill to bring her out of the bag, that everyone was able to feel the benefit of this little dog's presence. That was one of the wonderful things about Smoky: just knowing she was there was a comfort and for many crews she became a good luck talisman at a time good fortune was at a premium.

When preparing to board for another thirteen-hour mission, Smoky decided to turn her last 'relief' break into a dash across the runway. It was 3 a.m. and pitch black but she could see where she was headed. Bill ran about 500 feet before he caught up with her and gave her a piece of his mind. He wasn't really angry with her for running free, he understood that she probably realized what lay ahead and it's possible she made up her mind that she would rather just play in the grass. She was a dog, after all. Bill was not really angry with her. His anger came from the thought that she could have strayed under the wheels of a plane or an airfield Jeep and been killed. For the rest of the crew, Smokey's reluctance to fly was interpreted as an omen. When Bill had Smoky held firmly under his arm, he climbed the ladder into the belly of the Catalina. The crew stared at him and his dog in silence. Was it a bad omen? Did she delay the take off for a reason? Maybe it was to protect them from something awaiting them up there? Maybe the delay was important and prevented them being caught up in a storm of the dreaded Black Rain? Whatever it was that caused Smoky to run that morning and however superstitious the crew felt, it showed one thing: Smoky was considered one of them and she was important to each and every crew she flew with.

Smoky became something of a celebrity amongst the Catalina crews, particularly 3 ERS who flew with her those twelve times. Bill no longer had to keep her a secret from everyone but it was still essential that she was safe and secure during the flights when Bill had to concentrate on taking those crucial shots with the K-24 aerial camera. She spent most flights wrapped in a wool blanket to keep out the cold at high altitudes. It may not have always been the most comfortable environment for a dog but it was where she was closest to Bill and that was most important. This was a true partnership. Whether in the belly of a Catalina, at the foot of the US GI's cot or trudging through the New Guinea jungle, man and dog were together. Smoky flew because Bill flew and so everyone around them had the benefit of the dog's calming company.

Bill always used his non-flying time to teach Smoky some new tricks and he decided that he could teach her to ride a scooter. So, with just a few clever moves with his

Bowie knife, Bill constructed a foot-long scooter out of a wooden orange crate. Pulleys and roller bearings salvaged from the engineers doubled as wheels. It was a runaway success. Someone found pots of red and white paint from somewhere and painted the scooter red with white wheels and the name Smoky along the footplate. The scooter and Smoky made their debut before a small but appreciative crowd of GIs on Biak Island. This sublime scene was to be recalled in sharp contrast against the turn the war was about to take for Smoky and for Bill.

The gravel-throated hum of the Catalina's engines echoed in Bill's head. It was a sound that had become so much a part of him that even a moment of silence was deafening. One mid-October afternoon, as the crew were heading back to Biak, Bill was trying to think of something other than the engine noise when he caught sight of a massive fleet of warships. Through the shifting cloud he could see the convoy heading in the opposite direction. Immediately, the pilot dipped the Catalina's wings to show that it was friendly and just in time too as two Navy Corsairs swooped in to challenge them. Bill could make out battleships, cruisers, carriers and destroyers. The vast movement of naval hardware just kept moving and from the air it seemed the translucent blue of the Pacific was being swallowed-up by a dense pall of gunmetal grey. It took thirty minutes for the Catalina to pass over the naval convoy from beginning to end. Bill later discovered that the ships were heading for Leyte Gulf where they would engage in what was acknowledged by many as the largest naval battle in history.

The Battle of Leyte Gulf took place between 23 and 26 October 1944 and comprised four distinct engagements all fought off the island. It featured the largest battleships ever built – the Japanese *Yamato* and *Musashi* – who actually engaged each other in the battle. It was also the first time the Allies had encountered Japanese kamikaze aircraft. The pilots were young and zealous and ready to experience honour in death. The Battle of Leyte Gulf had been a long time coming. Since the Japanese sent their carrier-based aircraft to attack Pearl Harbor in December 1941, the United States of America and the entire Allied Force knew the Emperor had a plan of action. In fact, he had two: one for the east and one for the south. For the east, Pearl Harbor would be followed by the taking of the Philippines and then Guam and Wake to stifle the American communication system. In the south, he would attack Malaya and Hong Kong and then launch a systematic bombardment of the Bismark Archipelago, Java and Sumatra. This would then leave New Zealand and Australia totally isolated. For some months, the Japanese invasion of the Philippines looked impossible to stop. On 8 May 1942, the 80,000 soldiers of the US and Philippine Army were ordered to surrender the islands.

It had not helped that the US had divided their control over military activities in the Pacific. General Douglas MacArthur had been appointed Supreme Allied Commander South West Pacific. Meanwhile, the US Navy was under Admiral Chester Nimitz, giving him control of the rest of the Pacific Ocean. Two great men with one immensely hard job to do. The surrender highlighted the need for the Allies to pull together. By the time Bill Wynne received his call papers in Ohio, the tide had turned for the Japanese.

The skill of the code-breakers was critical if the US Forces were to be one step ahead of the enemy. Discovering an imminent attack on Port Moresby in New Guinea, in May 1942 Admiral Nimitz rushed the aircraft carrier *USS Lexington* to join the *USS Yorktown* and the American–Australian Task Force with orders to confront the Japanese attack. Port Moresby could not fall to the enemy. If it did, Japan would have control of the seas to the north of Australia. What followed was the Battle of the Coral Sea: a naval battle fought between the aircraft based on the carriers. The carriers did not meet or exchange fire but the damage they caused was enough to send the Japanese into retreat. Although at great losses, the Allied victory secured Port Moresby.

The Battle of Midway in June 1942was to prove critical in the Pacific War. The Japanese had relied on superior gun power to win over the opposition but this sea battle was about superiority in the air and the US claimed that advantage. The Japanese were then unable to force a ground battle leaving the US Navy calling the shots. The Japanese Navy was feeling the strain of not being able to repair and replace its hardware as swiftly as the Americans. All over New Guinea, the effects of these battles were being reflected on land. By late 1942, the Japanese were retreating in the highlands of New Guinea and with the assistance of Australian Forces the US was able to capture the Buna-Gona beachhead in early 1943. This had been a key position for the Japanese invasion. The Allied leaders of the Asian and Pacific Theatres – Chinese leader Generalissimo Chiang Kai-shek, US President Franklin D. Roosevelt and British Prime Minister Winston Churchill – met in Cairo to discuss the way ahead with Japan. In June 1943, the Allies launched Operation Cartwheel which defined the strategy for the South Pacific. The plan was to starve the Japanese out of their base at Rabaul and sever the communication lines. This prepared the way for Nimitz's target to reach Japan or at least get close enough to launch a series of strategic air attacks to facilitate invasion. The Allies' movement across the Pacific seizing one island after another was underway. The use of submarines in the Pacific War had previously been underestimated. Now they became one of the single most powerful forces capable of crippling the Japanese. US subs were responsible for destroying 56 per cent of the enemy's merchant ships. Mines and aircraft were responsible for the rest. They were used in reconnaissance and, as in the Battle of Midway had sighted the enemy fleet approaching giving the Allies the advantage. They were also responsible for saving many lives, especially of downed flyers.

When 128,000 US Army troops and Marines landed on the island of Saipan on 15 June 1944, the objective was to create the airfields that were to send B-29s over Tokyo. The plan had been devised over ninety days and it had to work because it was imperative the Allies secure the island. It was equally important to the Japanese Commanders to retain it. And to do this, they would have to destroy the US Fifth Fleet which comprised 15 carriers with 956 planes, seven battleships, 28 submarines, 69 destroyers and several cruisers. Admiral Raymond A. Spruance was in command. The opposition, under Vice Admiral Jisaburo Ozawa was outclassed and outnumbered by the Allies. But this battle was all about strategy and the one advantage Ozawa had was that his fighter planes were lighter than the US Navy Hellcat and therefore had a greater range. By positioning his fleet 300 miles out, he could attack the US carriers, land at Guam to refuel and then hit again. It could have worked if the planes had not arrived in staggered sequence allowing the US Hellcats to pick them off. Nimitz's carriers had individual combat information centres and were onto the

Japanese plan right away. The Emperor's Navy was virtually destroyed. And Saipan was in US hands.

When General Douglas MacArthur waded ashore at Leyte on 20 October 1944 he was flanked by the Sixth United States Army. His landing had been the result of successful bombardment by air and sea which cleared the way through. While the Sixth Army continued its advance from the east and the enemy tried to re-enforce their position from the west, the US Fifth Air Force was able to stop the Japanese attempts to resupply. Even though, by 7 December, the US Army was in control and the Allies had cut off the Japanese ability to supply Leyte, fierce battles were still taking place. Neither side was going to let go of their prize easily. It was into this background that Bill and Smoky went into battle.

Around the same time Bill saw the convoy of ships heading for Leyte, he received news that he was due combat leave having notched up seventy-three hours flying time in thirteen missions over ten weeks. He had been expecting a response to his application for promotion but this news was just as good. He packed for ten days R & R in Sydney and hitched a ride on a Transport Command C-47. Of course, Smoky took leave too as there was no way Bill would go anywhere without her. But their break was not to be the restful time they had hoped for – man and dog still managed to have a few adventures.

One night, while sheltering from a storm with several friends, Bill chose the right place to stand. Suddenly there was a loud crack and crash! A huge tree had fallen on the group and pinned several people to the ground – all except Bill, who was the only person to escape unhurt. Recounting the story to a tail gunner from the Jolly Roger 90th Bomber Group, the man told him: 'You are being saved for a bullet!' A part of Bill believed that too. There were so many times the ending could have been so different but somehow the good luck kept running on.

As it did the afternoon Bill was walking with Smoky at his heels in the streets of Sydney. Chatting to his friends, Bill looked down to check on his dog only to find that she had disappeared. Horrified, he looked around and saw a woman walking away with Smoky under her arm! 'Excuse me, but you have my dog,' said Bill. The woman insisted the dog was hers. 'She's been mine for a long time in New Guinea, Ma'am. You'd better give her back to me – right now!' Reluctantly, she handed Smoky over. Smoky gave Bill a huge lick on his face as if to say, 'Thanks Dad!' It was the last time Bill let Smoky walk at heel in public again.

When Bill returned from leave, the squadron was awaiting orders. There was a general air of anxiety hanging over everything as news of General MacArthur's landings on the southern beaches of the island of Mindoro filtered through the ranks. The landings had taken place in a key location in the planned Lingayen Gulf operations and were to support the major landings on Luzon. It was to Luzon that Bill and Smoky were headed. Loading Landing Ship Tank (LST) 927 with supplies and equipment was physically demanding. Everything had to be stacked deep on the tank deck of the ship and it had to be done quickly and accurately.

Everyone had been recalled to the squadron and all flights grounded except for the pilots of the F-5 recon planes which had to be flown to the next station. Bill and his colleagues knew very little about what was to happen to them but they were proudly aware that 26th Photo Recon Squadron was the only recon squadron going to Luzon. They had been chosen for the mission and would be going in the second invasion convoy behind the Navy assault ships and landing forces and would hit the beach after the combat troops had taken sufficient territory inland. As a precautionary measure, fifty personnel from each ship were swapped between the two convoys: fifty from Bill's ship, LST 927, were transferred to 391st Night Fighter Squadron on LST 706 and vice versa. Bill and Smoky were among those swapped onto the first convoy and Bill knew that meant strict army rations of dehydrated food and having to find a bunk amongst all the hardware for Smoky. The area below deck had room for 260 men in bunks and hammocks but it was very cramped. Bill decided to put his cot on deck between the army vehicles. It seemed to be the lesser of the two evils. Besides, other members of the 26th were in the hold, directly below, and that area could be easily accessed if needs be. Just nine feet away from a 20 mm anti-aircraft gun and four feet from an air vent, it was not going to be a quiet spot but that was the least of their worries.

As soon as they were out at sea, Bill opened the musette bag and allowed Smoky to stroll on deck. No one minded and everyone seemed interested in how he found Smoky and how he had taught her all her marvellous tricks. Every day Bill would let her wander the deck to meet her adoring fans and, more than anything, enjoy some much-needed exercise. There was another canine mascot aboard ship, a Dalmatian who wore a life belt around his middle in case he fell overboard. Smoky and her spotted friend got along famously and many a soldier and sailor had their photographs taken on deck with the dogs as they all made the long journey to Luzon.

For Smoky, being aboard ship was a whole new experience. She accepted the new smells of engine oil, rust, salt, disinfectant and unwashed soldiers. She also had to get used to going without a bath. Exposure to the salt air and water made her coat coarse and brushing against the rusty chains striped her coat a dirty orange. Catching the tail end of a typhoon, the ships pitched and rolled in twenty-five-foot waves. Sometimes, the swell of the water would momentarily take the ships from view as they made their way up the west coast of the South Philippines through the Mindanao Sea, the Sulu Sea and the South China Sea. Sometimes, only able to move forward at ten knots, it was a slow journey.

Daily drills on deck and preparing for battle kept the men busy. The decks had been cleared of the canvas shelters that were an obvious fire hazard in an attack and the greatest fear was the ship being hit by a kamikaze plane – this had happened to one of the ships ahead of them. As the sun was going down off the coast of Mindoro, life aboard the ship was normal: some of the men were playing cards, others sleeping on their cots. Some broke the rules by drafting a letter home – although they knew it could not be sent, maybe it made them feel closer to their family. Suddenly the general quarters was sounded and everyone jumped to their duties. The gunners dashed to their stations and others tumbled helmets and jackets into place. Army personnel were ordered below decks as a sailor ran through closing the bulkhead hatches. From there, they had to stay closed. Everyone understood that if they were trapped in a damaged compartment, the hatch would not be opened. An eerie quiet spread through the ship. After ten minutes, the horns and bells of general quarters sounded again and this time the action was for real.

Bill grabbed Smoky and returned to his cot between the truck and the Jeep. He hit the deck and pulled Smoky in close to his body, cupping his right hand over her ears. The ship's guns opened fire. The twin Bofors guns on the bow and the two 40 mm guns that flanked them thundered into action. The gunner and loader at the 20 mm anti-aircraft gun next to Bill were loading and firing repeatedly; their target was a group of eight planes coming out of the grey cloud. The ship rocked violently in the water as the guns pounded. Smoky's fragile body juddered with each shot fired. Bill held her as close as he could and whispered words of reassurance: 'It's OK, girl. Don't you worry now … everything will be fine …' Over and over he said the words that he hoped would also provide some reassurance for him.

Though there was gunfire, smoke and shrapnel all around him, it was somehow natural to look to the sky to make sense of what was happening. Holding tightly to Smoky, Bill scanned the clouds and there, right above him, two kamikaze planes were diving towards him. They looked on target for the guns which were blasting back into the sky. As his boots scrunched on the pieces of shrapnel scattered on the deck, Bill watched as one of the planes disappeared off the ship's bow and the other hit a Liberty ship to the left. A jet of water stretched into the sky as the first plane cut its nose into the waves and smoke billowed from the stricken Liberty ship. The noise was deafening and Smoky shivered in fear.

The all clear finally sounded and it was time to assess the damage. The first shell had hit the ventilator, passing over Bill's head when he hit the deck by the Jeep. Those who were standing there were hit. If the shell had hit two inches lower, it would have killed Bill and Smoky outright. Was that the bullet he had been saved for? Despite the creeping darkness, the gunners remained on duty and it was a blessing they did as another kamikaze plane hit that night.

What took place in the battles of the Mindoro Sea was something Bill and his fellow GIs would never forget. Continuing in convoy, they eventually reached the meeting point in Lingayen Gulf where the huge fleet awaited their orders to go ashore. The days and nights were never free of the noise of rifle fire as the men shot at something or nothing in the water, in their nervousness over what lay ahead.

On 9 January 1945, General Krueger, Commander of the Sixth Army, landed his first units on the western coast of Luzon. Almost 200,000 men moved across the 20-mile beachhead over just a few days. With support from the air, the army units marched in land. Krueger expressed annoyance that the 26th Recon Squadron was not in operation. Within days, they received their order to 'Hit the beach'. The order had come through in the middle of the night and by dawn Bill and the rest of the soldiers aboard LST 706 were wading through the waist-deep water to walk the forty feet to the beach. Once out of the bow doors and down, Bill struggled with barrack bag over his shoulder, carbine in hand, cot in the other and Smoky under his arm. As they headed for the beach, other crafts were arriving, opening their bow doors and dropping the ramps for the men to run out. They met little resistance as the Japanese had not expected them to land at that point. Ten US divisions and five independent regiments battled on Luzon. It was the largest campaign of the Pacific War involving more US troops than were sent to North Africa, Italy and the South of France. Bill took a chance to grab some rations from the stockpile on the beach. He put some tins of peaches and meat in his bag knowing they would come in handy because no one knew what was going to happen next. After the tide went out, Bill and the others returned to the LST to retrieve the vehicles. Driving the Jeeps and trucks down the ramp, the red alert sounded. Bill gathered Smoky under his arm and took cover. An ammunitions dump had been hit and sheets of fire leaped into the sky.

Smoky was happy to be back in a Jeep and on the road, even if the roads were really only bumpy tracks. All the supplies were loaded onto the beach and dispersed from there. Meanwhile the priority for 26th Recon was to construct the E2 building as the photo laboratory was needed right away. Driving through the local villages, the evidence of warfare was all around with stone debris lying everywhere. Some of the local people broke away from their clearing up work and waved to the US soldiers. Out in the countryside, the paddy fields and nipa houses lined the route to Lingayen, the provincial capital eighty miles northwest of Manila where 26th Photo Recon had taken over a full office block. To reach this block, they had to negotiate the bulldozers and trucks operated by the combat engineers working hard to repair and prepare the airstrip. They were laying steel matting over the runway and the taxiway which lay just a mile away from 26th Recon's new HQ. The 391st Night Fighter Group were camped down nearby but Bill and his colleagues decided to save time on setting up tents by moving into the empty local houses. The bamboo structures had roofs and sides made of palm leaves which kept out the heavy rain. A ladder stood at the entrance to each house so the upper rooms could be reached: the area under the house was where the chickens and pigs were kept. The bamboo floor was a danger to Smoky as her little feet could easily slip through the slats so Bill Smoky-proofed the floor by sliding a flat board under his cot so she could move around without getting hurt.

The local people were very supportive of the soldiers as they set up their accommodation. There was always the hope that they would receive payment in food as there was very little left to eat after a visit from the Japanese soldiers as they had passed through. Bill had seen some of the villagers taking food scraps from bins to feed to their families. When it was decided the soldiers should leave the locals' houses and return to their tents, the villagers offered to help in the move and carry out some of the practical tasks in return for food and American dollars. It was a plan that worked very well for everyone. The food and the work and payment changed the lives of the locals who had been left with nothing. But this was still a war zone and the nightly explosions and hails of gunfire were a stark reminder of reality amongst the palm trees and the sand. Every time the red alert sounded, Bill knew he had to cup his hands over Smoky's ears to muffle the sound. She was very nervous now and Bill was afraid that if he let her go, she would run away in fear.

The aerial photography was becoming more and more vital to the strategy of the war in the Pacific than ever before. Each day, a specially assigned pilot flew sets of prints collated by 26th Recon to MacArthur's command post and to his generals. Admiral Nimitz and his fleet commanders received sets of images too. There was a general feeling that they were part of something bigger. It was not the first time they had experienced being under attack but it was the first time they had worked directly with the front line. The twenty-four-hour shifts at the photo lab put everyone under immense pressure so having Smoky there as a happy distraction was very welcome. She worked the same shifts as Bill and, when possible, Bill would do extra shows for the guys on the opposite shift. Smoky cheered everyone's day.

A visit from Sergeant Bob Gapp from the Communications Section revealed a serious problem at the airstrip. 'We need to get our telephone lines through a drainage culvert – it is eight inches wide and runs sixty feet under the taxiway,' said Gapp. 'I saw a newsreel where a cat did that in Alaska … and it seems Smoky is a smart dog and, I thought, maybe we could coax her through the pipe?' He went on to explain that if Smoky could do this it would save days of work removing the steel matting, digging up the culvert, putting in the wire and reversing the process. If Smoky could do this she would, potentially, be saving lives and equipment.

But would Smoky go down the narrow pipe? Bill wanted to know just two things from Gapp: Could you see light at the other end of the pipe? And if she got stuck would they dig her out? Gapp confirmed both and on that basis only, Bill agreed to give it a try. They leapt into the sergeant's weapons carrier and headed for the front line. The idea was to slip a length of lightweight string through Smoky's collar; something that would break if she became caught. She would have to go down one of three drain culverts which sat side by side. Bill checked them all out and discovered only the middle one was straight enough to see light through to the end. Leaving Gapp with Smoky, Bill moved to the other end of the pipe but just as they got into place one of the new US fighter planes, the P-51 Mustang, taxied over the steel matting. The sound was deafening and poor Smoky shook in Gapp's hands. Several P-38 engines were being turned over at the same time and the noise was just too much for Smoky. Her little body quivered as the noise shuddered through her tiny frame. Bill could sense this but he had to give this a try. Men's lives were at stake here.

Eventually the engine noises stopped and Smoky was given time to calm down. After about twenty minutes watching Smoky's progress, Bill and Sergeant Gapp decided it was time to go. 'Come, Smoky, come,' Bill shouted. He could make out a shadow of the little dog's body at the entrance to the pipe. Her instinct was to turn back but Bill called again, 'Come, Smoky, come.' Smoky turned immediately and made her way down the pipe towards Bill. Bill's heart was in his throat. All the time he was wondering how he could put his friend through this task. She had to cover sixty feet from start to finish. But a quick check on her as he looked down the pipe reassured him that she was fine and heading in his direction. 'Come Smoky, come! Come on, baby, come on!' he called. The string was still being fed through the tunnel so the men knew she was still moving ahead. Then, suddenly, Bill saw the amber of Smoky's eyes just a few feet away. 'Atta girl! Atta girl,' Bill shouted. 'She's here!'

Breaking into a run, Smoky threw herself into Bill's outstretched arms. Sergeant Gapp hurried over and pulled more of the line through before cutting Smoky free. Smoky had been promised a steak if she made it through the pipe and within a minute of Smoky emerging from the pipe, Gapp was on his way to fetch it for her. If ever a dog deserved a steak, it was this dog. Smoky's action that day was a supreme addition to the war effort and the moment she accomplished her task Bill was aware that his dog's status in the Pacific had been catapulted from mascot to war dog.

As war dog and all-round celebrity, Smoky was able to draw in big crowds whenever Bill put on one of his shows. With the help of his buddies, Bill constructed a small stage from bamboo and palm leaves for the performances which ran before or sometimes after the main picture at the camp cinema. Walking the tightrope, rolling along on the oil drum, playing dead were all part of Smoky's repertoire as the raids became less frequent.

But the war was not over. Bill and his colleagues in the photo lab were still working flat out to provide the combined forces spread all over Luzon with prints showing enemy positions. Being one step ahead of the enemy was always the plan for regaining the Philippines from the Japanese and consequently many battles were fought and many lives lost on both sides in the process. It was a war of great personal loss and great tragedy. The sanctuary of the environment during its peaceful moments was the salvation of many. The sunsets and the balmy evenings became treasured parts of the day.

Bill asked the local seamstress to make some additions to Smoky's coat: 'Smoky Champion Yank Mascot SWPA 1944' was added with a blank patch beside it for any future campaigns. A local carpenter was tasked to make a platform, ladder and sliding board for Smoky's performance. The mahogany pieces were a genuine work of art. And so was the artistry of the squadron painter who continued the circus theme to match the other pieces Bill had brought with him from Biak, but this time adding the insignia of the 26th Photo Recon Squadron which featured Donald Duck in a red flying helmet and yellow scarf on a cloud perch shooting with an aerial camera. Walt Disney had personally donated this design for the squadron. Smoky now had a full range of circus-themed equipment – now all she needed was a costume. For that, Bill had to look no further than the seamstress who rustled up a clown costume and others from remnants of a parachute.

Smoky was a very clever dog and that was not always evident from her stage act. It was the little things she did which impressed Bill more. If she was thirsty she would go over to the bag of drinking water in the centre of the squadron area and then catch the first passerby. By running between the man and the water and barking at the water bag she always managed to get her drink. Bill was very happy for Smoky to be everyone's friend but he dissuaded people from teaching her new tricks as he did not want her to be confused over who was her master. In Bill's mind, discipline was his territory alone and on more than one occasion her training saved her life. One day, when she was following another dog over a road, he came within inches of losing her. Fortunately she reacted immediately to Bill's very loud, 'Stand! Stay!' And the truck rumbled by without doing anyone any harm. But it was a close call – Smoky had cheated death by no more than six inches.

Always feeling there was room for improvement when it came to the tricks and to discipline, Bill gained permission to use a house next to his tent as a rehearsal hall. As before, he covered the slatted bamboo floor with a sheet of plywood to safeguard Smoky's feet and set about adding to the repertoire of tricks and refining the old favourites. He tried out a new combination act which involved jumping through a hoop and also introduced Smoky to the idea of spelling out her name in large cardboard letters. This became Bill and Smoky's early morning routine before the 37°C heat of the day set in. And it was worth it. Bill really felt the show was ready to go on.

The day President Franklin D. Roosevelt died, a nation mourned and Harry Truman took on the mantle of President of the United States of America and Commander-in-Chief of the military. The troops looked to him to bring the war in the Pacific to a swift and satisfactory end.

The realities of living in a war zone were often too close and Smoky and all the other adopted menagerie of animals were constantly under threat from the heat and various diseases which could descend suddenly and kill within days. The moment Bill got wind that there was another threat in the camp, he isolated Smoky from every other creature in the place. Bill was disturbed one morning at about 3 a.m. by the sound of digging. It turned out that it was his friend Frank Petrilak and another friend digging a grave. The small, deep hole in the earth was for Smoky's pup Topper. He was only six months old when he died. The disease claimed the lives of thirty squadron dogs in one week. Only four survived; Smoky was one of them.

On 5 February 1945, a 1st Cavalry American tank liberated over 3,000 prisoners of war being held at the Santo Tomas internment camp. The crew opened the gates with a blast from the tank's guns and the prisoners, mostly American, poured out. They were the first Americans in the invasion force to land on Manila. Tears of gratitude and relief lined their faces. It seemed appropriate that the

Red Cross should move onto the site and transform the former prison camp into a general army hospital. It was also appropriate that the Red Cross send an invitation to their old friends Bill and Smoky to come and entertain the patients. Bill and Smoky wasted no time in boarding a truck bound for Santo Tomas where they were welcomed with open arms by the Red Cross nurses.

Taking very little equipment with him, Bill was still able to put on a show for fifteen wards. Each time, the show was a standing ovation success. Walking through the legs (the grapevine), playing dead and singing a few old Forces favourites brought smiles to many faces, providing the kind of medicine you cannot buy in a bottle. Photographs were taken and Smoky was interviewed on American Red Cross in Manila radio.

Back home, Bill's beloved Margi was able to see her man and Smoky in the newspapers and hear them on the radio. Others in the squadron started to receive letters from loved ones saying how they had seen the wonderful mascot dog, Smoky, on the news and once again Bill had a celebrity on his hands.

The war in Europe was over but it continued on Luzon where the casualties of the war were evident every day. In the North, a 40,000-strong Japanese Force was defending this slice of the Philippines. It was reported that the American losses on Luzon were high with over 8,000 killed in action, almost 30,000 injured and 157 missing. Japanese losses were higher at over 170,000 killed. The campaign on Luzon was indicative of the way the war was going. And for Bill and Smoky, the American advance on retaking territory from the enemy meant a move out to Okinawa to assist the planned invasion of Japan. It was July 1945 and the men and dogs of 26th Photo Recon Squadron were being briefed by their commanding officer ahead of being shipped out.

'We must strip ourselves of many personal possessions,' they were told, 'and no animals will be permitted to go.'

Bill's heart sank. But he need not have worried. Smoky's reputation as a war dog was as well known as her profile as mascot.

'… All except Smoky. She has been with us a long time as squadron mascot and she doesn't take up much space.'

Many of the men still smuggled their own pet friends aboard the troop ship but it was good for Bill to hear that Smoky was so highly regarded that she was now an official passenger and he no longer had to think of ingenious ways to stow her aboard. After distributing their belongings amongst the local people who had been such good friends and neighbours, the GIs boarded trucks bound for the docks and ships that would take them to Subic Bay where they would join the rest of the convoy awaiting orders for the invasion. A United States submarine guarded the fleet and smoke screens clouded the view of them from the sky.

Okinawa, along with Iwo Jima, had witnessed some of the fiercest fighting in the Pacific War. The Japanese increased the use of kamikaze planes in an effort to save their experienced pilots for other offensives. It also achieved their other goal – to inflict maximum damage on the Allies. Over 10,000 American Marines and sailors were killed on land and in the water surrounding these islands. The more the Japanese refused to surrender, the more strategic the bombing of Japanese cities became. Under the US Army Air Forces General Curtis May, sixty-four cities were destroyed by B-29 firebombing raids.

But the kamikaze planes had done their worst against the Allies and the mood on Okinawa was sombre and uncertain; no one knew what was going to happen next. All Bill knew was that he had to keep Smoky safe and happy until they could travel home to Cleveland, Ohio. Standing in the chow line, the only certain thing was that it would be bully beef on the menu. But that was always fine for Smoky. No one would ever hear a complaint from her about food, she just ate whatever she was given. As the men joked over their mascot's eating habits, Bill noticed a yellow teletype message fluttering on the notice board. The message said that one B-29 Superfortress had dropped an atom bomb on the Japanese city of

Hiroshima. An estimated 45,000 people had died as a result. More teletype messages came throughout the day and the men were told how the American planes had dropped leaflets telling people to evacuate the city but the Japanese had refused to agree to an unconditional surrender. Two days later, a second bomb was dropped on Nagasaki.

On 15 August 1945, Imperial Japan surrendered to the Allies. The formal instrument of surrender was signed on 2 September 1945 on the battleship *USS Missouri* in Tokyo Bay. The surrender was accepted by General Douglas MacArthur as Supreme Commander of the Allied Powers and representatives of several other Allied nations. MacArthur remained in Tokyo to oversee the post-war development of the country. But for the soldiers on the ground, there was a lot of work still to do and thousands of people to get home – including Bill and his devoted Smoky.

The war was over. In Okinawa, Bill and his fellow GIs felt honoured to be a small part of the peace process. From their campsite, they witnessed the arrival of the Japanese envoys on Le Shima. By order of the US Army, the white bombers would have large green crosses painted on them and be accompanied by six P-38s. From Okinawa they would fly to Manila and board the *USS Missouri*. Standing with Smoky under his arm watching this historic moment, Bill could feel the fear and anxiety of the past two years start to ebb away. When the P-38s came into view someone close to Bill shouted, 'It's over! Damn – it's over!' Bill laughed, feeling the relief of it all. He held Smoky close to his face and she gave him the biggest of kisses. The hand grenades that lined the barbed wire fence around the camp were removed. There was no need for them now. As the reality of the surrender began to sink in it automatically brought thoughts of home.

Leaving behind a traumatic part of your life can bring both elation and sadness. The joy brought by peace was undeniable but the recollections of friends lost in action was sometimes unbearable. Casualties incurred by 26th Photo Recon Squadron were among the highest in the 5th Air Force Recon Squadrons: thirteen dead, ten wounded or injured. Those who did make it through were thanking whoever they prayed to for keeping them safe. Bill and Smoky included.

Once again, the Red Cross sought out Bill and Smoky to perform for the troops. Bill was determined not to let anyone down this time. It was his last chance to show the men what Corporal Bill Wynne and Corporal Smoky could do. The performance at the servicemen's recreation hall was a hands down success and every trick, old and new, was performed perfectly. It was a good way to celebrate peace and comradeship and the contribution of the little dog who meant so much to so many people. The timing was perfect as everyone was destined for different postings. Most of the 5th Air Force was going to Japan. Some were going back to the States and others, including Bill and Smoky were assigned to Korea. A long ocean journey lay ahead and that was something he was not looking forward to. Instead, Bill decided to stay behind with the other dog owners and fly out later and there was still a great deal of work to do before they could leave Okinawa. The photo lab, E2 building, was left intact but the supplies were destroyed. Bill's friend John Hembury was still there with his dog, Duke, and another GI, Zeitlin, was there with his adopted sickly puppy and Smoky had developed a sinus problem so a vet's service would have been really really helpful. The 4th Marine War Dog Platoon was based less than a mile away so Bill decided to walk there in the hope that there would be a vet on site. The medic on duty came up with a cure for Smoky's sinus problem: a mixture of fresh milk and eggs. Before he left, Bill decided to take a look around the kennels. He wanted to meet the other war dogs, all of whom had experienced a war far more violent and disturbing than Smoky's. Bill was told about the one German Shepherd whose master had been killed in a foxhole; the dog had refused to leave the body. One of the soldiers managed to get the dog to move, but he had to beat him to do it.

At the mess hall, Bill was faced with powdered eggs and milk, but nothing fresh to give Smoky. It was all he had so he gave it a try. Smoky lapped it up without a murmur. For three days Bill continued with the mixture and, like a miracle, Smoky recovered.

The outcome was not so good for Zeitlin's sickly puppy. His shakes and convulsions were getting worse and everyone was convinced that he should be put out of his misery. So, with great emotion, the three men set about their sombre task. They tied the puppy to a post at the bottom of a hole and then Zeitlin took out his pistol. It was over in seconds. In silence, the men shovelled earth over the tiny body.

The trauma of war was over but there was always the force of nature to contend with in that part of the world. A typhoon was due and the remaining men had to tie everything down. When the winds hit at 11 a.m., the tent stood up to the test. By 5 a.m., the wind direction changed and everything was swept into the sky – including Smoky. Bill was carrying his cot with Smoky on top when the wind took both, spiralling into the air. He caught the cot and Smoky, trapping the cot against a wall to stop it taking flight again. Sheets of corrugated metal sliced through the air and everyone kept their heads down as they staggered to take shelter in the mess hall. Typhoons always came in twos and the second hit with a force of wind and rain that kept everyone wet for days.

The island was littered with caves and this seemed a good time for Bill and Smoky to check one of them out. They had to be the perfect shelter in a storm, after all. Bill knew that some of the caves were used as family tombs so wasn't surprised to find a selection of ceremonial pots laid out inside. He felt slightly awkward moving them but he needed to make room for himself and Smoky to lie down. What seemed like a good idea at the time turned into the most disturbed night's sleep Bill had known for some time. Smoky sensed something in the cave and had fits of barking all night and Bill could hear voices. They were happy to get back to the mess hall for some peace and quiet. There was a general sense that it was time to go and so Bill and the others decided to hitch a lift to Korea on any plane going. Most of the C-46 cargo planes were damaged in the typhoons but there was one with wings intact that was flying out that day. Bill and Hembury, Smoky and Duke made sure they were on it and bound for Seoul.

Bill and Smoky landed at Kimpo Airfield to discover their squadron had been billeted in barracks vacated by Japanese troops. It was October and the new accommodation felt luxurious in comparison with their digs in the Tropics. An escort Jeep had transferred them to their new temporary home, deep in the countryside. The cold was as difficult to live with as the intense heat of the jungle had been. The copious blankets and the two pot-bellied stoves in the dorms were a godsend. Smoky hated the cold and spent most of her time in Bill's arms or in his cot. Korea was now a holding station for US servicemen waiting to receive the long-awaited order to go home. There was time to fill and as always Bill used some of it to teach Smoky new tricks. In tidying his bag to make room for a few Japanese souvenirs (swords, bayonets, rifles and pistols were on offer) he rediscovered the large cardboard letters that he had made to teach Smoky how to spell her name. He took it as a sign to try it all over again. But this time Smoky had a surprise in store for her master. He might have tried to fool her by mixing up the letters for her to find but this time she was on the ball. S-M-O-K-Y ... there it was, every letter selected perfectly. Bill was so proud and there was a round of applause from the small but appreciative audience. Bill hugged Smoky so tight that he left her in no doubt that he was delighted with her performance which she repeated again and again each time to a standing ovation.

On the way home, Bill's main fear was concealing Smoky for the journey. This time, a gas mask bag came in handy and with some adaptation – zippered openings back and front – Smoky was able to practise going in and coming out of the bag to order. Bill wanted to take most of the show equipment back home too but the new barrack bags were not made with transporting circus equipment in mind. It was one bag per man and that was going to be difficult for some. Orders to depart came and went for Bill and Smoky but finally on 1 November 1946 it was their turn. Bill wrote home to say they were lining up for their last serving of army chow – it was quite a moment for the men and, if Smoky had realized the significance of the moment it would have been for her too, especially as all the meat she had known for the past two years was bully beef from a can. Getting to the US would mean a whole new life for Smoky and a new diet too. But first she had to get aboard the troop ship which was due to leave at 7 a.m. The excitement in the camp was almost tangible. Bill was understandably nervous – after all, army regulations stated, 'No dog or mascot will go back to the US on a War Department ship.' It was that clear. And it was the clarity that scared Bill the most. But he had a plan and Smoky had the routine in hand so he could not do any more. When the call to move out came at 3.30 a.m., Bill and Smoky were ready for their breakfast of pancakes and salty bacon before joining the horde of jolly GIs ready to board the collection of motor pool trucks waiting to take them to the Air Corps meeting point. From there they would change trucks for Inchon Harbour.

Bill spent the twenty-five-mile journey to the harbour worrying about Smoky. For weeks he had heard how some dogs had been ordered to stay behind and others thrown overboard when discovered on a troop ship. And she wasn't the only mascot being smuggled out. The big dog, Duke, was with Shorty Randall, as Hembury did not have a home suitable for such a big pet. Another GI had a monkey in his ammo box. To help bolster Smoky's case, Bill had a collection of photographs showing her visiting hospitals, with the men around the camp and entertaining the troops. Maybe all of this would allow this special dog to travel home in peace. Lining up to go aboard the landing barges, Bill handed his friend the bag with Smoky hiding inside. The man had hurt his back so could not carry his barrack bag but he could hold Smoky. She was wearing her specially adapted turtleneck jumper made from a sleeve so she would be warm for the journey. As the launches approached the troop ship *USS General W.M.H. Gordon* it dawned on them that they were really going home. Now was the moment of truth. He watched Randall stagger with Duke in his arms as they transferred from the launch. The officer in charge was shouting something but Bill could not hear what and feared the worst. Moments later, he saw the same officer gesture Randall to board the ship. Bill breathed a sigh of relief. All he needed now was for Smoky to stay still as his friend Piwarski took the bag through. Everything was going fine until Bill stumbled. He dropped one of the barrack bags but just about managed to trap it between his knees. Everyone was eager to get aboard and Bill was heckled to get a move on! The officer moved forward to help and in all the confusion Smoky came aboard without a hitch. The sleeping quarters were three decks down, so taking Smoky back from his friend, he went in search of the bunk furthest away from everyone and let Smoky out of her bag for a scamper on the bed. Few people knew Smoky was on board and Bill wanted to keep it that way until they were well out to sea. It took all night to load 5,000 men and their equipment.

Eventually they set off, the horn sounding their departure. Not far out to sea, the weather turned and the ship was tossed on the waves like a toy in a bath. Bill could not find his sea legs and for the next three days out of the twelve-day journey he was unable to eat or sleep. He heard that Randall had been summoned to the troop commander's office and told to take his dog ashore. Fortunately, the ship's captain was a dog lover and intervened before Randall was forced to carry out the orders. It turned out the crew had a few stowaway dogs stored safely below decks. Now Duke had joined the lucky ones. But it wasn't all over for Bill and Smoky yet. The ship's address system bellowed: 'All men on board who have brought either dogs or monkeys, report to the ship's office immediately.' It seemed that their time was up and Bill felt too ill to put up a fight.

Five men stood before the troop commander. 'No dogs and especially no monkeys go back on this ship,' he said. These dogs had meant so much to their individual units that the men were not going to let this beat them. The troop commander had tried all he could to put the men off but it did not work. It just made the men more determined than ever.

By chance, Smoky was seen by a Navy lieutenant walking around below deck. He asked to see her master and then her papers. Surely this was the moment Bill and Smoky's luck would finally run out. But no, with an agreement to pay the bond and to sign an oath stating that the *General Gordon* was cleared of any responsibility for the dog, they got away with it. It was a very lucky break as all the pet monkeys were put to sleep and only the dogs allowed to sail on.

The rest of the journey was more enjoyable than before and Bill felt well enough to put on the odd show or two to make the journey go much faster. Duke was allowed on deck every day and Smoky enjoyed scampering around with him as they had always been great friends. She would miss the big, old dog for sure. The *General Gordon* had been at sea for twelve days and, as they passed the islands of Puget Sound, they knew their journey was almost over. Local people brought out their tiny boats to meet the mighty ship that was bringing the troops home. The order came to disembark and Bill knew that he would be carrying Smoky off the ship this time and so reorganized his bags accordingly. His souvenir Japanese rifle and bayonet could go in the barrack bag and Smoky would once again be safe in the green bag with the straps and flaps. She knew her way around that one and its familiarity would be safe and comfortable. As the men queued up and through the ship, Bill reflected on the past two years and how a terrifying time had been made bearable only with the company of his little canine companion. As he strutted down the gangplank leaving behind the last piece of territory that linked him with the war, Bill was hit with the thought that he still did not know where Smoky had come from or how she had found herself in the New Guinea jungle and who had scripted the chain of incredible events that brought Bill into her life.

The *General Gordon* had brought them safely from Korea to Washington State to receive a heroes' welcome. No one bothered them for paper or bag checks or anything other than to welcome them home. The GIs were loaded onto trucks and they sped through the streets of Tacoma and on to Fort Lewis. They were then sorted into sections suitable for their final destinations and assigned a bed in the US Army barracks. After two years on a cot in a tent, this felt like something approaching home comforts. There was fresh milk and steaks waiting for them and Smoky sampled a little of each before settling down on Bill's bed for her first sleep in America.

The next morning there was a reunion with the rest of 26th Photo Recon who had travelled on an earlier but slower ship. The guys were pleased to see Smoky had made it through all the red tape and was destined for a home in peacetime. They were saddened to hear that Duke had not made it. Randall had lost the dog in Fort Lewis. No one knew the details but they did know that Randall was distraught, as one of the 'men' Duke had endured so much for so long. Bill looked to the sky and thanked whoever it was who was looking after Smoky. They knew they were the lucky ones.

The processing and the medical checks took four days to complete but at least the surroundings were pleasant and there was more fresh meat and milk for Smoky to enjoy. The troop trains had been waiting for them; Bill and Smoky were bound for Camp Atterbury, near Indianapolis, the closest separation centre to Ohio. Soldiers from all divisions of the Army came together on the trains: infantry, signal corps, the tank corps; they exchanged experiences and dreams for the future in a way that men feel they can only do in such extraordinary circumstances. For Bill, the future was clear. He was going home to Cleveland, to set a date to marry Margie. He had telephoned his mother with strict instructions not to tell Margie he was so close to home as he wanted to surprise her. Standing outside Margie's front door, with Smoky under his arm, he knocked. Bill, tall, dark and handsome in his new olive drabs with Eisenhower jacket (his first new uniform in two years), opened the door and let Smoky into the living room. He heard Margie's voice and could have cried. Smoky trotted up to Margie as if to say 'hello'. They were home.

What followed for Smoky was a life of adoration, decoration and total showbiz. Once the press in Bill's home town of Cleveland heard that he was back and with a hero war dog there was no stopping them printing all the stories they could about this little hero of the war in the Pacific. Just a week after arriving home, Smoky's story was splashed across the front page: *Tiny Dog Home from the War!* It had stolen column inches from the news of General Yamashita's death sentence. Many times over, Bill was to tell the story of how he had bought Smoky for the equivalent of six dollars, flown twelve combat missions in Catalinas between Biak, Borneo and the Philippines with Smoky beside him. How she had saved the airstrip on Luzon and how she had been a friend to all throughout their two years serving through to Okinawa and Korea. There were the awards too – Yank Magazine's SWPA Mascot 1943 was just one of them.

Her special coat made from a green felt card table cover was bursting with medals. On the day they received their discharge papers, Bill not only received his civilian train money and mustering out pay, but he also received the due recognition of all who served as members of the 26th Photo Recon Squadron – the Asiatic Pacific campaign ribbon and eight battle stars, the Philippine Liberation Ribbon with Battle Star, the Victory Medal with Battle Star and the Good Conduct Medal. A Presidential Unit Citation Ribbon with Oak Leaf Cluster was accompanied by silver crewman wings. Smoky wore those too.

Arriving home to a place she had never known before, Smoky made good friends with the pets Bill had left at home: Lucky, a big, black and very intelligent cat and Toby his loyal dog. Bill was afraid that Toby would have forgotten him, but after a few puzzled looks and a quiet time just listening to Bill's soft voice, it was as if he had never been away. They were old friends to Bill but new ones to Smoky and a new family for her too.

Smoky's new career included more hospital visits and travelling around to give shows. Providing the same kind of therapy for the injured soldiers now back home was a great comfort and Bill's pioneering work with Smoky as a therapy dog provided a good template for this as an activity in the US. Bill also returned to the orphanage at Palmerdale to give a show and received loud applause. His visits showed the sincere and valuable connection between animals and their ability to heal.

Hollywood beckoned and as members of the Hollywood Animal Handlers' Association Bill and Smoky made their big break on television in a programme called *Castles in the Air* which demonstrated Smoky's fondness for dressing up. Bill got in on the act too with their dog and tramp act and the song, *Mr Pokie and his Dog called Smoky*.

Bill retired from show business in 1954 taking Smoky with him. They were tempted back for the *How to Train your Dog with Bill and Smoky* show, which ran for an extended thirty weeks in 1954.

Smoky died as all fireside heroes should, in the arms of his family. On 21 February 1957 Bill came home to find his 'little pal lying on her side, asleep in death.' It was agreed that she should be buried in a special place and there was none more special than a spot in Cleveland's Metro Park under the tree on which Bill and Margie carved their initials in a heart one day in 1940. 'Our tree' was close to a clearing that Bill felt the perfect spot to lay Smoky to rest. Her tiny body, placed in a shoe box, was lowered carefully into the ground as the children wept over the loss of their little friend. Bill found it hard to hold back his own grief but knew he had to for his children. As he gathered stones to mark the grave, Bill thought of the times he had walked with Smoky in the New Guinea jungle and how they had entertained the troops bringing joy to a place that seemed incapable of witnessing laughter. This dog was a survivor. She was Smoky. The subject of six memorials in America all in praise of her huge bravery and unfathomable devotion.

Bill wrote, 'After I lost my dog, Pal … I felt so heartsick and vowed never again to get that close to anyone, animal or human, again. But Smoky, the little tyke who shared so much with me, who, unquestioning and courageously responded to my every command, had become my truest friend.' (From *Yorkie Doodle Dandy* – by William A. Wynne)

Antis –
Loyal Unto Death

'There is an old belief
That on some solemn shore
Beyond the sphere of grief
Dear friends shall meet once more.'

(Inscription on the grave of Antis at the PDSA Animal Cemetery in Ilford,
North London, by John Gibson Lockheart)

As friendships go, there are few that could rival the mutual devotion of Czechoslovak pilot Václav Robert Bozděch and his dog, Antis. It was a relationship born out of war, strengthened as a consequence of war and one that came to rest in peace beyond war. The Alsatian had spent eleven of his fourteen years on Air Force bases in France and Britain and if a dog is capable of storing memories he would have recalled the happy days he spent with No. 311 (Czechoslovak) Squadron and how he saved Bozděch's life a thousand times over in so many ways.

Born in Bohemia in 1912, Bozděch had a happy, though poor, childhood. He excelled at every level of his schooling and went on to perform well at technical college. Here he was heavily influenced by the Czechoslovak emphasis on physical fitness. An eager and dedicated student, Bozděch selected athletics and handball as the sports he would excel in and in his spare time, to satisfy his love of music, he learnt to play the accordion. By the time he graduated in 1929, he was a well-rounded young man with many prospects and a bright future. His technology-based course had given him all he needed to begin working as a locksmith but the obvious limitations of the job soon began to frustrate this intelligent young man and he was relieved when his call-up papers arrived for his two years' compulsory military service. All young Czechoslovak men considered it an honour to serve their country in this way and the timing was perfect for Bozděch. For him, the time away from normal routine was an opportunity to reassess his future. He had never considered a career in the military but now he could see how his technical know-how could be advanced in this environment. The experience also came at a time when he was becoming more aware of his country's politics and the fragility of Czechoslovakia's independence in Europe. The way he saw it, if his country was destined to be an innocent pawn in a political power struggle between France, Britain and Germany then there was probably only one way he could defend and serve his country and that was in uniform.

Two years' compulsory service gave him an opportunity to test the military waters. Following basic training, Bozděch decided to put his technological knowledge to good use and became a mechanic in the Air Force. Two years later, after demobilizing, he went to work for the car manufacturer Skoda but thoughts of his time in the Air Force stayed with him. In October 1937, unable to ignore these thoughts any longer, Bozděch rejoined the Service and trained as an air gunner.

Adolf Hitler had made no secret of his desire to occupy Czechoslovakia and the same year Bozděch joined the Air Force, Germany's leader prepared to invade his homeland. Although Hitler had assured the Czechoslovak people that he would protect the German-speaking regions of Bohemia and Moravia, President Beneš was not convinced his country would survive the might of the Third Reich. As an insurance policy he had built up the Czechoslovak Air Force and looked to his allies for reassurance that they would stand shoulder to shoulder against the German threat. Czechoslovakia's primary protection was her pact with France but there seemed little confirmation that the terms of their agreement would be upheld if the threat of invasion became a reality. And how would Britain react if France went to war with Germany?

The threat to Czechoslovak freedom had become universally apparent. In an attempt to resolve this territorial tug of war, a meeting was arranged between Italy, Britain and France and Adolf Hitler's Germany. Munich was selected as the venue to reach a settlement. Ironically, Czechoslovakia was informed it would not be required to attend. On hearing the news, the Czechoslovak Minister, Dr Jan Masaryk, commented to British Prime Minister Neville Chamberlain, 'If you have sacrificed my nation to preserve the peace of the world, I will be the first to applaud you. But if not, gentlemen, God help your souls.'

The Munich agreement failed. Czechoslovakia was alone. On 1 October 1938, German troops entered the Sudetan area, commandeering over 1,600 Czechoslovak Air Force planes and sending the country's army into withdrawal. By 13 March 1939, Hitler was threatening to bomb Prague unless his Third Reich was allowed to take over Bohemia and Moravia as Protectorate. By 15 March, as the snow fell in the early morning, a convoy of German armoured vehicles snaked through these long-defended communities and by evening Hitler was in Prague. President Beneš had already left for Europe with a plan to set up a democratic government in exile. Even though Germany had jackbooted all over the democracy he had cultivated over the previous twenty years, the defiant President would not accept that it was over.

For Bozděch, it was time to leave his homeland and, with his typical dignity, strength and belief in truth, secure a plan to win it back. Alongside thousands of other army and air force personnel, Bozděch began to plan his escape route. So far, the West had failed to show itself to be a trustworthy ally. The allegiance was there on paper but France and Britain had failed to come through for the Czechoslovak people when they needed it most and Germany had them backed against the wall. Action was required but it was not provided. But who else was going to be in a position of strength and capable of stopping Hitler in his tracks? Only Western democracy was in a position to do that and had any chance of achieving success. Now it was just a matter of being in the right place should war be declared on Germany, which to many people war looked inevitable.

Bozděch, like many others, chose Poland as his destination and plotted a journey through northern Moravia and on to Ostrava. His home in Bohemia would be the start of his 300-mile trek on foot and he planned to set out once the harsh winter had passed. He applied for leave, rather than just disappearing which would have attracted the attention of the Gestapo. The last thing he wanted was to have them hot on his heels. Leave papers in hand, he travelled on public transport to his home in Soběkury, to say goodbye to his family.

He had very little money and what he had paid for food and public transport only when it was absolutely necessary. It took him ten days to reach the border and by the time he reported to the reception camp in Male Bronowice – where all Czechoslovakian airmen were directed – he was penniless. Once there and amongst Czechoslovakian friends who had also run the gauntlet to escape German rule, he was able to talk freely, bathe and feel easy taking financial help.

Poland was a stop-gap and not the place where Bozděch and many of the others planned to stay for long;

they were welcomed but there was no great call for air force recruits. He heard that the French were happy to absorb the men and so on the last day of July 1939, with a visa issued by the French Consulate in Krakov just three weeks earlier, Bozděch arrived at the port of Calais. He was one of 470 Czechoslovakian airmen who made for France on six ships between May and August that year. They arrived ready and willing to fight for democracy, for justice and for the freedom of those imprisoned by Hitler's Third Reich.

But before they could sign up, there was a political hurdle to clear. If the French allowed the airmen to join its Air Force unconditionally, the outside world could misconstrue this as a threat. To avoid this, the French issued a policy that all Czechoslovakian airmen sign a standard five-year contract with the Foreign Legion. To serve France now meant they could also fight their own battle for Czechoslovak freedom later on – under the conditions of the contract, in the event of war breaking out, the soldiers and airmen could transfer to the Czechoslovak units serving under the French military. It was a little more than a spoken promise but in their powerless situation it was enough to send the men into action with a zeal for justice.

After signing up, they were shipped out to the Legion's base at Sidi-bel-Abbès where they relinquished their individual ranks for the one rank of soldat. The

Czechoslovakians distinguished themselves from the others by their sheer focus and ability to adapt; they marched and fought proudly earning the respect of the French officers and men alike.

On 1 September 1939, Germany invaded Poland. It was the catalyst for Britain and France to launch their defence against Hitler's march through Europe. Two days later, they declared war on Germany. For Bozděch and his compatriots the start of the Second World War was their cue to take up arms as Czechoslovakians, this time attached to the French Air Force. Once the transfer had taken place, a period of refresher courses followed and, eager to get on with the job of war, Bozděch passed each one with flying colours. He had one priority and that was to get back into the air. He completed courses in mechanics and gunnery and also trained as a wireless operator. Once back in the air, the men felt they had control again and, as the Czechoslovakian airmen's contract with the French had said, they could now bond with their own units and fight under the banner of their country. Now they felt they could make a difference and stall Germany's grip on Europe.

It was at this point that Bozděch met the dog that was to change his life in so very many ways. Fate or whatever it is that dictates these things, put the man and the dog in the same place at the right time and there it was – pure serendipity. Bozděch's bomber plane was returning from a raid over Germany when it crash landed in a field close to a ruined farm house. They were in no-man's-land, caught between the French and German border. Bozděch and his navigator staggered out of the wreck and tried to get their bearings. They had landed in the middle of nowhere. Lost and in danger, they decided to walk in search of civilization, their handguns at the ready in case they walked into trouble. A few minutes later, they stumbled across a small farmhouse that had been left in ruins following a German bombing raid. Suddenly, the silence was broken by a rustling sound coming from the fallen masonry. Immediately, the men reached for their guns. Gradually closing in on the area, they realized the noise was actually a whimpering, snuffling sound. The men weren't sure if it was human or animal but they had to investigate. Bozděch narrowed the sound down to a corner of the ruined house and there in front of him stood a small black and dark tan puppy with the most enormous ears. The dog's soft brown eyes were full of fear and he looked at Bozděch as if to say, 'So, are you going to shoot me?' Of course Bozděch was not going to shoot the dog, even if part of him thought it would be the easiest thing to do. This dog was going with them. In one bold move, the airman lifted the dog from his hiding place and placed him inside his flying jacket, the dog's head nestled next to the airman's chest, his heartbeat comforting the puppy who must have been more terrified than his rescuers.

There was no time to hang around. With the plane ditched it was up to the men to find their way back to the airfield. As they walked and hitched their way, Bozděch spoke softly to his new companion, cradling the little bundle in the palm of his hand so he could not slip down inside the jacket. The lilt of the man's deep voice and the mutual body warmth of man and dog began to work its magic. The puppy relaxed a little and by the time the new recruit reached his new home he was fast asleep.

Bozdech's fellow airmen were impressed with their friend's find. The puppy was very accommodating and sat still and quietly while the men looked him over. They quickly decided that he had to be an Alsatian. The disproportionately large ears were quite a talking point and the conversation quickly turned to the task of giving the dog a name. Everyone wanted to take their turn with ideas; even though it was assumed from the start that the dog belonged to Bozděch, the animal was going to be living with everyone and so everyone wanted to be involved. The ideas for names ranged from the wild to the silly but then one man suggested something so good that it was perfect. 'What about naming the dog after a plane?' he said. The Czechoslovakian Air Force had bought PE-2s from the Russians and called them ANT. The men could not have known how totally appropriate the name would turn out to be. Most importantly, the dog seemed to like it. Every time the men tested him, 'Ant! Come here, Ant!' his huge ears would reach for the sky, his head would drop to one side and his tongue would loll out of his mouth. But from the start Ant, later lengthened to Antis, decided that he was not going to take orders from anyone other than his rescuer. Someone else may have called his name but Antis would immediately look to his master before doing any other man's bidding. The bond was already starting to develop.

In the early months of 1940, Antis was a happy dog who enjoyed all the privileges of being an airman's companion – lots of attention, scraps from the men's tables, plenty of people to play with. Antis was playful and attentive and, although clearly Bozděch's dog, he was happy to mingle in with everyone and very soon considered himself one of the crew. And Bozděch decided to make it official – it was the best way he could think of for keeping man and dog together. His training came to an end in May 1940 and he was transferred to an active section right away and started taking Antis with him. The dog lay at the gunner's feet and soon realized he could sleep the whole time he was in the air. Taking Antis on the sorties was vitally important to Bozděch as he didn't want to risk leaving him behind and then find the dog had been transferred away without him, or worse. It was a time of great confusion as the Allies rallied to stop Germany's rampage through Europe. The German Panzer divisions were driving into France, Calais fell and the evacuation of British Forces began at Dunkirk. If General Von Rundstedt, the German Commander in Chief of the French campaign, had not decided to halt the Panzer columns in order to protect them, this part of the campaign may not have gone so well for the Allies. As it was, the withdrawal of the ranks meant more time to move the men out of Dunkirk. Then all efforts were focused on saving Paris from the clutches of the Germans. But things had gone too far; Parisians were packing and leaving along with the Belgians from the north of France. Refugees littered the road although they really did not have anywhere to go. By 14 June, the German occupation of Paris was complete.

The Czechoslovak airmen were left in a state of uncertainty. The political movers and shakers in their own country were trying to use this situation to manipulate a better deal for their men who were split between sixteen squadrons in the French Air Force. The advice at the base had been for the men to pack their belongings and head for Tours. Bozděch, his dog and the eight other airmen in his group decided to make their way to Blois instead, managing to commandeer a horse and trap along the way and then boarding a train which was packed with refugees. With limited rations to take with them, there was very little for the men or Antis to eat.

The safety of British territory seemed too far away for comfort and scant news and direction did little for morale. The War Office in London worked hard to remain in communication with the Czechoslovak servicemen – they had been promised British transportation out of occupied France but this was now impossible to guarantee. The way out was going to be a long and tough route via North Africa. For a man now so determined to save this foundling dog and take him wherever he was going, the next three weeks would be quite a challenge. Arriving in Gibraltar on the last day of June, they were almost home and dry. Transferring to a transport ship, even third class was luxury compared to the variety of vessels they had taken during their journey so far and they bedded down for the next leg of the voyage which would take them into Dover.

Bozděch and his dog settled into a space on deck near the stern. It gave them time to reflect on the journey so far and to make a plan on how to get the dog through the British quarantine regulations. It was obvious the authorities would be on the lookout for animals being smuggled out and even though there might have been some sympathy for a soldier risking his own life to protect his dog's, it was not going to help Bozděch right now. It was against regulations and that was that. Through the ship's officer and an interpreter, the men were told the consequences of not abiding by the strict quarantine laws. If they could pay the fees it would help the animal's safe passage into the country. If not, the animal would be humanely destroyed. There was only one thing to do – smuggle the dog all the way through to disembarking in Liverpool.

When the ship docked there was a great deal of confusion. The Czechoslovakians, along with other foreign servicemen who were all under the command of their own officers, mingled with the British soldiers and government personnel as the paperwork was sorted out. Everyone was in a rush to get to where they were expected to be and were not overly interested in anyone else's problems. The men were lined up on deck and filed down the gangplank as their bags were collected and loaded onto lorries. There was only one bag that Bozděch was eager to get his hands on – the one that hid Antis. He lifted it slowly, softly singing under his breath, and made sure it was loaded onto the lorry. That left only one more hurdle – the kit bags were to be stacked on the station platform. Bozděch's heart was in his throat. Antis had played along with his plan perfectly until then but was this too much to ask of the puppy? With bags loaded on top of him and around him, how could he keep quiet if he was hurt? Fortunately, Bozděch was not alone in this plan and everyone else who knew what was going on was aware of the immediate danger of Antis being discovered. They listened intently. Then they heard it – a whimper. A quick-thinking airman decided to join in with a very convincing act of a dog whining to go home! The man was a well-known joker in the group and so the display didn't attract suspicion or the attention of the police or the officers. The men laughed and the police smiled and soon the bags were on board the train bound for Liverpool. For now, at least, Antis was safe.

The men and their dog were bound for Cholmondeley Park, a majestic country estate in Cheshire. Cholmondeley was the designated camp for the Czechoslovak Army and Air Force and the location for the reuniting and redeploying of the Czechoslovak servicemen. The men had pitched their army-issue tents all over the grounds and they were welcome to do so. There was enormous respect for the Czechoslovakians from the British, thanks to their loyalty, strength and stoic endurance. Maybe it was a reputation built on a history of periodically having to fight for their rights. And here they were doing the same again, giving their all to the Allied cause. In 1939, they saw their own country fall to German occupation but instead of breaking them it only made them more determined than ever to win.

Bringing the Czechoslovakians together at Cholmondeley was the catalyst for the formation of the Czechoslovak Squadrons of the RAF, something the men were incredibly proud to be a part of. On 22 July, during a visit from the exiled Czechoslovak President, Dr Beneš, the airmen were officially recognized as part of the RAF. The soldiers marched alongside the airmen in the parade and saluted them as they left the ground to prepare to take to the air once more. This time they would fly as Czechoslovakians under British control with the British Government officially recognizing them as allies and their homeland as the Provisional Government of Czechoslovakia in Exile.

Located in rolling countryside a few miles outside Wolverhampton in the industrial West Midlands, the modern airfield of RAF Cosford was to be home to Antis and Bozděch for the next two months. There they would spend their time training, learning the basics and the most important elements of the English language and then they would get back in the air. For this stage, the men relinquished their ranks in the Czechoslovak Air Force and Bozděch was no longer a sergeant. For the duration of his training he would be an aircraftsman. And Antis? He had to learn to be patient and wait for his master to emerge from the classroom. And he would be there every night waiting for him. The training was run to a very strict timetable so it didn't take the dog long to key in to the time he could expect to see his master at the end of the day. From the moment he saw Bozděch off in the morning Antis would set about finding breakfast leftovers in the canteen. Any snacks and attention could be easily found by visiting the nurses at the hospital on site or befriending the Women's Auxiliary Air Force

(WAAFs) who loved to see Antis and made sure he had plenty of attention.

Antis was now a big puppy and, like most teenagers, he was all legs; when he ran his feet went in all directions. His head looked too big for his body and his ears still looked far too big for his head. He had all the physical indications of becoming a big dog and a handsome one too. His sable-coloured coat was short haired and it looked glossy and healthy. He had a lovely temperament and didn't mind people approaching him; he would always greet people with a bright-eyed expression and with eager anticipation of getting plenty of attention. He took every encounter in his stride and was happy as long as no one was threatening his master.

The bond between man and dog was already firmly cemented but Bozděch knew that he had to teach his dog some manners if he was going to be accepted wherever they were posted. A dog on an airbase was not at all unusual but with everyone living so close together the dog had to be sociable. That was why, after the airman finished his day's training in the classroom, he would start Antis's training in the barracks. He could tell from the start that his dog was intelligent and eager to learn all that his master had to impart. Bozděch thought back to his childhood for guidance on training dogs. Growing up in a rural community, he had seen men take dogs and train them for duties on the land and he remembered enough of what he had seen to put it into practice with Antis. The dog reacted well and was as well-trained as any dog could be in the basics of canine etiquette. But there was one thing that could not be eased with time or patience and that was the anxiety the dog suffered when his master had to leave him on the ground. Antis was inconsolable. It was something both man and dog would have to get used to – or so it seemed that way at the time.

The movement of air crews was now critical. More men and planes were needed to take on the German Luftwaffe. By September, it was time for Bozděch and Antis to be transferred to Duxford Airfield where they would join No. 312 (Czechoslovak) Squadron in Fighter Command flying in Defiant aircraft. They were waiting for a consignment to be delivered and spirits were high in anticipation of the operations that lay ahead. But as Hitler changed tactics and began bombing British cities and innocent civilians, No. 312 Squadron was relocated to Speke Airfield in Liverpool. Night after night, the city was subjected to aerial bombardment. One night, Bozděch and Antis found themselves in the thick of the action.

After visiting his girlfriend in the city, Bozděch was walking with Antis when the air-raid warning sounded. Running out of time to reach the shelter and with bombs overhead, Bozděch took Antis in his arms and hit the ground. Protecting his dog's body with his own, the airman lay still. The sky flashed orange with the mass explosions raining down from the German bombers. Wave after wave of them droned overhead and it seemed as if the noise would never stop. On and on it went and man and dog opted to lay low until it was all over. Gradually, the noise of people's voices started to emerge from the darkness and confusion. Torch lights flashed and swirled around as the all clear sounded. Bozděch raised his head from the floor and a cloud of dust made him choke and splutter. Antis's sable coat was white with masonry dust but he seemed alert and showed no obvious signs of injury, much to his master's relief. They picked themselves up off the ground and entered a new world of activity. The bombing had stopped but now the search for survivors was going on all around them.

Suddenly, Antis started whining. Bozděch established that the dog was not in pain but it seemed he had picked up on a scent or a sign that someone was in distress nearby. The Civil Defence Warden saw the dog's reaction and signalled, the best way he could, for the Czechoslovak airman and his dog to follow him into the centre of the search area. A huge heap of rubble that had, until moments before, been several homes loomed ahead of them. With torn clothes and dust-covered faces, the survivors desperately tore at the bricks. Someone's loved ones were under that pile. They could hear them shouting and they had to reach them before it was too late.

Antis moved into the crowd of people and started digging. Suddenly, he stopped still and started barking. He would not move from the spot. Taking the hint, the men started to dig. The rescuers found four people – alive. Within seconds of that find, a wall collapsed close to them covering the area in chunks of cragged masonry. For a few moments, Antis was lost from Bozděch's view. The bricks and the dust obscured everything for a moment and then, just as quickly, cleared to reveal the dog standing above the heap, barking. He was alerting the party to what might have been a bedroom and looking down on a cot with a baby inside, a woman close by, her arms outstretched. Both had perished.

It seemed like a very long night to Bozděch and he was concerned about Antis who looked weary. It had all been a new experience for this dog who was really only little more than a puppy. But the noise of the planes was something he was getting used to and the dog was a hero. Arriving back in camp covered in dust and his uniform in tatters, shoes torn and useless, Bozděch told the others what Antis had done on the streets of Liverpool and the lives he had saved that night. Antis himself had fallen fast asleep and was blissfully unaware of the praise that was being heaped on him. The snoring hero had never slept a deeper sleep.

Sleep, deep or shallow, was a luxury many had given up a long time before they reached Liverpool. But the incessant bombing raids – over 150 by the end of September – made rest impossible. Each plane had its own noise and after a short time the airmen could distinguish between an Allied and an enemy plane. They could even identify the exact model of the planes passing overhead. As soon as the engine noise entered the sky, the men automatically tuned in to it and quickly distinguished if it was friend or foe. One September night, a lone plane passed over Speke Airfield, its engine wide open. A Czechoslovak airman detected the change in the sound as the plane dipped and dashed at low level over the hangars. 'Get out! Get out of the hut!' he yelled. The telltale pattern signalled that the plane, a Dornier 217, had dropped a stick of bombs.

Bursting through the doors of the hut, the men ran for the nearest air-raid shelter by the NAAFI. The hut they had left was in flames and running from the fire they attracted the hail of bullets from the plane's machine gun. The men took to the floor as the search lights and anti-aircraft guns burst into action. The noise was deafening. Antis ran with the men for a while and then disappeared from sight. The Dornier inflicted maximum damage on the airfield, churning up the ground and destroying buildings. As the plane disappeared from the sky, the noise waned and a sudden peace fell on the site. For

Bozděch there was only one question: where was Antis? He called the dog's name over and over. Others joined in to help him but the dog did not appear. That night was the loneliest of any, for that one Czechoslovak airman at least.

As the airfield returned to normality, Bozděch realized he had fractured a bone in his hand. He used his recovery time to search for Antis. The dog had never left his side before and so it seemed sensible to start facing the fact that the dog could have been injured in the bombing raid and skulked off to die. One day ran into two days and this thought was becoming even more real. As he searched, Bozděch became more and more convinced that he was looking for the body of his dog and not an injured dog. Suddenly, the rain came with force, breaking through the dampness which had covered the airfield since the bombing raid and soaking the ground. Planes were unlikely to take to the skies in this weather but they still had to be maintained and made ready for immediate take-off if necessary. As a group of mechanics ran from the NAAFI to the hangars, one of them saw a dark, crumpled heap of something on the ground just ahead of them. He went to investigate although he expected it to be just another piece of mangled debris that had blown from the pile of timber and rubble that had been gathered after the attack. He never for one moment expected it to be the squadron mascot, Antis.

A call was put out for Bozděch who rushed to where the mechanic had brought the dog indoors. Already people were gathered around and their sadness was clear to the frantic airman as he approached. Though weak from his ordeal, Antis managed to raise his head as he heard his master's footsteps approach. He held his head off the ground for a fraction of a second before resting it back onto the floor. Just that small effort exhausted him. Bozděch spoke softly to his dog in Czechoslovakian, the language he first heard from his rescuer, in tones he would have remembered from the first moments they spent together in France. Bozděch put his face close to his dog's muzzle and stroked his head as he spoke in a quiet and comforting voice. For many of the Czechoslovak and British airmen watching, this was almost too much to bear and as they drifted away the dog's owner was left with the most tortured thoughts. If this was the moment that he would be taken from him then so be it, he thought. But the medics decided to take him into their care – the squadron mascot was going to receive the best chance possible.

As Antis was being cared for, Bozděch wanted to investigate where his dog could have been for two days and how he had survived. Piecing together the evidence from a tour of the airfield, the airman deduced that it was possible Antis had been thrown into a bomb crater during the raid and then, as he became weaker and more dehydrated, could not clamber out of the hole. The heavy rain provided him with water to drink and the small boost he needed to make a crucial move, a lifesaving move.

For the Czechoslovak airman it was time to make a move too. Antis's return had given Bozděch the resolve to make a request to transfer to No. 311 (Czechoslovak) Squadron of Bomber Command. He was now a qualified air gunner and his sergeant stripes had been reinstated so he knew he was qualified to serve with this illustrious Czechoslovak squadron. The request was granted and the same for two more of his countrymen – and their now famous, lifesaving mascot dog.

By October 1940, RAF Honington in Suffolk had the honour of training the Czechoslovak air crews to fly the mighty Wellington bomber. These great warhorses of RAF Bomber Command had already shown their might in the air and they would continue to do so throughout the war. With a six-man crew and the capacity to drop a bomb load of 4,500 pounds and hit at a range of 1,500 miles, the Wellington was a unique giant and irreplaceable in the ranks of RAF hardware. To the British public it was an iconic presence in the skies and wowed cinema audiences when it appeared on the pre-film news reels. The deep roar of a Wellington bomber ploughed pride into the heart of the nation and struck fear into the bellies of the enemy. This indomitable plane and the famously defiant Czechoslovak air crews were a formidable combination.

East Wretham Airfield, the satellite base of RAF Honington, where No. 311 Squadron was billeted, was a spread of huts and tents surrounding a farmhouse. This was where Antis and Bozděch bedded down with their fellow Czechoslovakians and enjoyed the distractions of a working farm amidst the chaos of war. This location was perfect for Antis to recover and he was well on the way to being his old self. He still suffered the odd setback when he heard gunfire or an explosion but was much stronger. The farmyard became his playground although he was strictly forbidden from chasing any of the livestock, especially the turkeys.

The atmosphere had proven the perfect setting for the Czechoslovaks' first Christmas in Britain and they were able to enjoy a party with all the trimmings. The festivities went so well that no one noticed Antis lapping up the leftovers in everyone's glasses. His wobbly walk and party-piece antics walking into doors and walls gave the game away and he was carried to Bozděch's bed where he slept a long, sound sleep before waking and drinking gallons of water. It was good that everyone was able to enjoy the respite of Christmas as January 1941 brought new challenges.

Despite their combined years of service in their own Air Force and since their arrival in France and then Britain, the RAF still regarded Bozděch and his fellow Czecho-slovaks as freshmen. Treating them as combat virgins was somewhat patronizing although having time to get used to the ways of a Wellington bomber was much appreciated even by the most experienced flyers. The handholding missions would often be conducted by Squadron Leader 'Pick' Pickard, the RAF Liaison Officer for No. 311 Squadron. He had great admiration for the Czechoslovak air crews and his inspirational approach drew mutual admiration from his students. By February, the men were operational with six aircraft heading out with a full quota of bombs. Their mission: to destroy the channel ports. Bozděch and Antis were part of a Wellington crew known as 1598-C – C for Cecilia. Dunkirk, Calais and Bremen were their targets and for the first time the crew of Cecilia felt the full force of the German anti-aircraft fire. Antis was on board, lying at the feet of his master. Throughout the gunfire, he obediently followed Bozděch's strict orders to stay still. The warmth of the faithful mascot dog against his leg was a comfort to Bozděch but his position as gunner was vulnerable and that made Antis vulnerable too. From the moment the airman had lifted the puppy from the ruins of the farmhouse, they had protected each other and now that bond was stronger than ever. Five of the six aircraft returned from the mission: Cecilia was one of the lucky ones.

The bombing raids continued throughout April with Bozděch taking part in five of the eight missions and, in recognition of this, he was awarded the Czechoslovakian Medal for Valour. A month later he added the Czechoslovakian War Cross to his collection. Antis was not going to receive any medals for flying because, even as the squadron's mascot dog, under RAF regulations he was not permitted to fly with his master. But he did fly, everyone knew it, unofficially, and as Cecilia survived raid after raid, the dog came to be seen as a good luck charm.

When they flew in France, the work was low level and there was no need for oxygen. But the Wellington bomber flew at a much higher altitude and so they had to provide Antis with an oxygen mask. Of course, it would have been easier to leave the dog on the ground but the last time Bozděch tried that it ended in disaster. Antis could recognize the distinctive sound of 1598-C miles before she appeared in the sky over East Wretham and as soon as he heard the first strains of the plane's engines he began to relax in the knowledge that his master would soon be home. In June 1941, during a raid on Hamm, the plane took a hit and was forced to land at Coltishall. In the attack Bozděch was struck on the head by flying shrapnel and had to be transferred to hospital in Norwich. For two days, Antis waited outdoors on the airfield for his master's plane to return. He refused to eat or drink and snarled at anyone who tried to distract him from his duty. Day and night, rain or shine Antis waited. Thanks to the squadron's chaplain, Bozděch was told what was happening and allowed to collect the dog from East Wretham and take him back to the hospital where they could share a room while the airman fully recovered from his injuries. After thirteen days, man and dog were ready to return to flying. Their next mission would be a raid on Bremen.

Somehow Antis had not only developed an ear for 1598-C for Cecilia's engines but a sixth sense for detecting when the men were preparing to leave. On this occasion, Antis was determined not to be left behind. He had learnt to climb the ladder into the body of the plane and, while no one was looking, he made himself comfortable in one of the canvas slings used for supporting injured crew members. He was safe and hidden and eventually fell asleep as the plane was being prepared for take off. Several hours later, as the flight passed over the Dutch coast, Antis was forced to show himself. He needed oxygen – and quickly. Feeling a touch on his arm, Bozděch turned expecting one of the crew but instead it was Antis. Surprised and pleased to see his dog, the airman realized the reason for his distress. As the dog's sides heaved and he struggled to take in air, Bozděch undid the straps of his own oxygen mask and held it to the dog's muzzle. Quickly changing position, he ordered Antis to lie between his feet where his head could be raised and the mask could be held over the dog's muzzle. The dog lay still and allowed this to happen, possibly realizing that it was all to help him breathe more easily. The plane was flying over Germany at around 15,000 feet and Bozděch needed both hands for the guns. Bozděch took the decision to fix the mask comfortably to Antis's muzzle while he could, in anticipation of the pilot needing to take the plane higher during the flight. Man and dog now had to share the mask. As soon as he could feel himself perspire and getting slightly lightheaded, Bozděch took a breath of oxygen from the mask and then replaced it on Antis. He knew they could carry on doing this for the duration of the mission and arrive home safely.

No sooner had Bozděch made the decision to share the oxygen mask and felt easier in himself than the plane ran into a violent electrical storm. As lightening struck, the plane's instruments began to fail. The men had only one option: to drop their bomb load over the sea and then to return to East Wretham while the bomber still had some engine power. The crew and the plane survived the mission but others from the airbase had not and the crew put this down to Antis's presence – he was their hero of the skies. He was now indispensable and from then each time the crew was called for a sortie all six men, plus an Alsatian, would appear for duty. And Antis would have his own oxygen mask and kit bag to take aboard.

Throughout June and July of 1941, the night bombing raids seemed never-ending and No. 311 Squadron was permanently on duty. There was some elation amongst the men when Hitler attacked the Soviet Union in his ill-fated launch of 187 divisions of the Wehrmacht. The Czechoslovakians had hoped they would be sent in to support their new ally and the idea lifted their spirits up and away from the drudge of the night missions that were proving so stressful and exhausting.

Bozděch's crew took part in bombing raids over Bremen, Hanover, Hamburg, Mannheim, Essen, Cologne, Munster and Brest and on 25 July 1941 he was awarded a bar to his Czechoslovakian War Cross. Antis was beside him each time, lying silently at his master's feet in the gun turret. He may have been the crew's lucky mascot but he was not immune to injury. In one of his first sorties a fragment of shrapnel pierced his oxygen mask and clipped his nose and left ear. He was clearly in pain but Antis did not whimper or complain.

Sometimes, the extent of his injuries only came to light when the mission was over and the dog was completing his usual victory romp around the airfield. After their final mission, over Mannheim, there was no victory romp as Antis sustained injuries that were beyond the endurance of most dogs. Cecilia had dropped her bomb load on target and was headed for home when she took a hit under her belly that sent her reeling in the sky. A barrage of anti-aircraft fire peppered the entire fuselage as the pilots fought to regain control. Searchlights highlighted the stricken bomber as it clawed at the sky to right itself. No sooner had the light picked them out, than a squadron of fighter planes emerged to finish the job. Oil splashed onto the pilots' faces and jets of cold air forced their way through the holes in the floor and the body of the plane. Cecilia shuddered under the impact of the constant firing but she was not ready to give up. When, at last, the sky fell quiet but for the Wellington's stuttering engines, the old warhorse had survived, lame and scarred but still with enough strength to get everyone home.

The pilot checked with all crew members in turn, asking each of them if they were all right. Everyone answered – they had all survived but nerves were on edge. They wanted to get home and the first light of dawn was a welcome sight as the aircraft thudded over the town of Thetford. For the first time in many hours, Bozděch felt he could allow himself to relax a little. Concentrating on the sky and what was happening outside the plane had taken its toll on him physically and emotionally. It was only as the smell of English meadows and the sweet earth started to clear away the stench of oil and cordite that home seemed a reality once more.

Throughout the mission, Bozděch had reached down and stroked Antis on the head to comfort the dog lying so obediently at his feet. The soft touch had always been met with a warm lick or the brush of the dog's muzzle. It was just enough to reassure each other that all was well between them. Nearing home, the airman's thoughts reached out to thinking about his dog and how patient and well-behaved he had been throughout the night flight and the air attack. Bozděch reached down to unfasten Antis's oxygen mask, giving him a stroke of appreciation. As he reached down, he saw the dog was motionless. Turning his lamp on the spot at his feet, the airman saw a pool of blood surrounding his dog. Falling to the floor to get a closer look, he could see a long, deep gash in Antis's chest. It looked like a shell splinter was to blame and the injury was now hours old. Bozděch later wrote about that moment saying, 'Never once had he tried to hinder or distract the men from their duty. Silently he had lain there, staring mutely at his master and bearing his pain with a fortitude not often found even amongst the bravest of men.' (*Freedom of the Air,* Hamish Ross).

There was no veterinary care on the base and so Bozděch carried his dog to the sick bay and prayed they could help him. With his head cradled in his master's arms, and thanks to the gentle handling of the doctor and nurse, Antis relaxed his grip on the pain he had controlled for many hours. The gash was severe and the dog had lost a lot of blood but there was enough spirit left in him to see him make a full recovery. The dog had everything he needed right there: his master, his friends and first-class medical care.

The rest of the crew waited patiently for news of their mascot's recovery. The dog had been the only one injured on that raid but the crew were exhausted and trauma-tized by the experience. The plane was badly damaged in the mission – it was full of holes and its engine had been pushed way beyond any expected limit. The only thing to do was to take it out of commission to repair it. The crew had grown so close in the way they thought, behaved and reacted that each loss was personal. It was a team and also a family, and even the aircraft was their friend and protector. She had certainly protected them this far. And as for their mascot: he was one of them too and they could feel his pain. But all they could do was wait. There was some doubt if Cecilia would ever be the same again but the big question was would Antis ever fly again?

The story of the stoic dog and the brave airmen hit the newspapers. For thirty-two sorties, the crew of Cecilia flew with their mascot dog at the air gunner's feet. What a story that was to make a nation's heart swell. The hand-some Czechoslovak airman and the Alsatian with a crooked left ear, hurt as a result of facing the enemy in the sky. Each time the dog's exploits were picked up by the newspapers, the RAF had refused to comment. Bozděch had slipped into the background, afraid that drawing attention to the dog's flight record would also highlight the RAF's disapproval when it came to dogs being allowed on war planes. The last thing anyone wanted was for Antis to be taken away. He was not only Bozděch's dog, he was the crew's companion.

A posting to RAF Evanton in Scotland placed man and dog in the spotlight. Bozděch was working with No. 8 Air Gunnery School to train future air gunners. His reputation with Bomber Command had preceded him and the RAF had decided that it was men with his experience who could bring new gunners through. The cadets, a mix of Czechoslovakians and Poles, would be put through their paces in the training room and in the air by Bozděch. Their respect for the man was obvious; they were in awe of the man who had completed thirty-two sorties and was now sharing that knowledge and experience with them. But off duty, the youngsters also wanted to meet the airman's heroic dog. Bozděch almost always shied away from the attention but Antis made up for any reluctance on his master's part and lapped up the attention. It was no surprise that in such a small community this man and dog made such a huge impression. Everyone knew them. In October 1942, in a local dog show in Dingwall, Antis won first prize in a competition for best dog handled by a member of the Allied Forces. It was an award that seemed made for this man and this dog. The newspapers certainly saw it that way too.

Following a flurry of interest in the dog show win in the local press, came mass coverage in the national press who had seen a much bigger picture: Here was a hero of Bomber Command who had rescued a puppy from a ruined French farmhouse in no-man's-land in 1940. And that same puppy was now a loyal and fearless war dog, having accompanied his master on thirty-two sorties over enemy territory. The RAF had tried to keep the story of the airman and the dog under wraps by merely sidestepping requests for information but now there was nowhere to go. The story was out there and now it was time to capitalize on one of the RAF's greatest assets – Antis, hero dog of Bomber Command.

Antis's position was now more secure than it had ever been. With such huge public interest, the RAF would have to protect their war dog. And they were soon called upon to do exactly that. Antis was charged with worrying sheep and the case was taken to court. Bozděch had to go to court to speak for Antis and he asked the RAF confirm his account of Antis's bravery under fire during his time with No. 311 Squadron. And the RAF told of how he had been injured but did not distract anyone from their duties and how his presence brought peace and comfort to the crew on every sortie they flew together. Antis's passion for chasing sheep placed him on death row but did the court really want to be responsible for shooting a war hero?

In the end, they decided to let it go with a fine. And the RAF came to see the publicity surrounding the dog as good for the Service and unrivalled public-relations material for the war effort. None of the reports mentioned the rule against taking mascots on missions and at this point in the war, boosting the morale of the people was almost as important to the government as battle strategy. Antis's exploits with Bomber Command had delivered the RAF exactly what they needed, a hero.

Bozděch was in demand in the classroom as well as in the air and travelled around the country in his new role. Antis took the relocations in his stride; getting to know new people was not a problem for him and as long as his master was with him all was right in his world. The freedom the dog was given on the airbases sometimes resulted in behaviour that disappointed Bozděch. On the rare occasions his master went into the local town, Antis would track him down, as he still hated to be on his own. Sometimes, he would link up with a group of cadets from the base and they would take him back with them or he would catch the local bus and the driver would make sure he got off at the right stop. One time, when they were stationed in Scotland, Antis caught the wrong bus and went so far off track that Bozděch had to arrange for him to have a lift back to base on a Botha aircraft. Somehow, luck always seemed to be on Antis's side and as people recognized him they always made the link with Bozděch and made sure he made it home. But there was one occasion when everyone was convinced the dog's luck had finally run out: the night he answered the call of the wild.

He was gone from base for five days. This was not like him and Bozděch was worried sick about him. When he was finally found, he was limping through the town of Evanton, thinner than ever before and bearing the scars of more than one fight. He was spotted by a group of cadets who, sure it was Antis, approached him carefully. But the dog looked nervous and wary and, as the men came closer, he ran from them taking a leap over a fence. As he jumped, he misjudged the height and was impaled on the spikes, badly scoring his stomach. Carefully, the cadets lifted the dog to safety and took him to the local vet in Inverness. After four days in their care he was transferred back to the camp where Bozděch watched over his friend for the next two months. The experience had traumatized both man and dog and it was a separation that neither was to endure again.

The postings in Scotland gave Bozděch a chance to walk and he took pleasure in the wonders of nature and wildlife – both pastimes he indulged in during his childhood in Bohemia. While based at RAF Evanton, Antis shared Bozděch's long walks and took any spare moment he could to be outdoors. But it wasn't until Bozděch was posted to the anti-submarine patrols at RAF Tain, in the north of Scotland, that Antis returned to his favourite place – at the feet of his master as they took to the skies once more. This time they were due to rejoin their old unit No. 311 Squadron assigned the job of flying Liberators with Coastal Command. It was August 1944 and the German U-boats were proving a great threat to the Allied operation. After D-Day, the Germans lost their U-boat base in France and shifted their focus to Norway who also had a very valuable store of fuel. By the time Antis and his master rejoined their old squadron in January 1945, it had been four years since they had last served with the now famous crew. Names and faces had changed and now some of Bozděch's trainees were coming through the ranks which was very rewarding for him. And of course they all knew Antis which made the experience feel like a homecoming.

Being operational again meant Bozděch worried about Antis. He knew the sorties could last at least eleven to twelve hours at a time and were subject to the extreme weather conditions so could be even longer. It was not always possible to return to Tain so if Antis was flying or waiting at the base it would be an anxious time for man and dog. But, however difficult for the pair, the operations had to be completed and Bozděch, with or without his dog, was one of the Liberator's crew of eight and had a job to do. He thought he should try to cure Antis of his separation anxiety by leaving him in the care of others and seeing what happened. It didn't work. The man pined and the dog pined and refused to eat. The airman had to admit that his experiment had failed and, as he wrote later, 'that all their mutual suffering had been in vain'. (*Freedom in the Air,* Hamish Ross).

On one occasion, Bozděch left Antis at the base and set out on a sortie. But once they were in the air, the weather turned and Bozděch's plane had to be diverted for several hours. When the Liberator finally touched down in Tain, Antis was too ill to come and meet the plane. He had taken to his bed and was unable to move; he could hardly bear to lift his head when his master appeared. Bozděch stroked his dog's furrowed brow and noticed his hard, dry nose. Taking him immediately to the vet, the Czechoslovak airman was told that his canine flying partner was now grounded due to kidney problems. If he were exposed to a long flight Antis would be in danger of losing his life.

As an airborne dog, Antis's career was virtually over but his role in the RAF was ongoing. During his time at RAF Tain, Antis passed an important milestone in his career as he was promoted from being a mascot to the higher status of veteran. Every visitor was introduced to the dog and told of his prowess as a war dog and his loyalty as a friend. In letters home to their loved ones the men often included paragraphs of Antis. Talking about the dog offered relatives a little light relief from the grey news of their war which was taking place under a grey sky and over grey water. It was a normality that most of the men wanted to communicate to the outside world. Particularly as the news from the outside world was making every Czechoslovak serviceman and civilian so insecure.

On 5 May 1945, a No. 311 Squadron Liberator made its last anti-submarine patrol of the war. The crew sighted a U-boat and immediately deployed five depth charges. The submarine took a direct hit and as the Liberator circled the stricken vessel, like a vulture on its prey, the crew witnessed a series of explosions before the hull of the U-boat appeared on the surface of the water surrounded by a spreading mass of oil. The Liberator's crew looked forward to being able to celebrate their victory on return. Little did they know that there would be more to celebrate than the sinking of the U-boat. That day the Czechoslovak Government appealed to the British Air Force to support an attack on the German troops and support the liberation of Prague. The crews of No. 311 Squadron knew the Liberators had the ability to reach Prague and, in anticipation of being given the order to support the Prague Rising, the crews slept in their aircraft so there would be no delay in answering the call of their homeland.

Throughout May, the politicians wrangled over the conditions that would allow the Czechoslovak airmen to return home. There were rumours that the Soviet Union was creating barriers although the Americans would claim they were responsible for the liberation of Prague with the arrival of General Patton's tanks on 7 May. The British took a frustrating middle-ground position which was ended, finally, on 11 June when Prime Minister Winston Churchill declared that the airmen could, at last, go home. Although more than content with the decision, Air Vice Marshal Janoušek, KCB was not content with the condition of the aircraft men would be taking back home. The Liberators of No. 311 Squadron were a contemporary design and would serve the Czechoslovak Air Force well, but the Air Ministry was embarrassed into replacing the Czechoslovak fighter squadrons with brand-new Spitfires. It was only right that this loyal band of airmen who had served the Allied cause so well should fly home in planes to match the pride they had in their country and their Air Force. President Beneš had been in Czechoslovakia since May and had made a triumphant entry into Prague. The Czechoslovakian Armoured Brigade was already home. All the country needed now was the return of its Air Force.

Antis, like his master, was a paragon of patience. For three months, the Czechoslovak airmen waited for the order to return home and when, at last, the day came – 13 August 1945 – the Liberators left RAF Tain for RAF Manston on the first leg of their journey home to Prague. Five years before, Antis had entered the country as a stowaway now he was leaving it as a war dog and a hero. The welcome home could not have been more fitting for the bold and the brave. The twelve converted Liberator bombers of No. 311 Squadron flanked by the fifteen new Spitfires emblazoned with fresh Czechoslovak Air Force markings, swept victoriously over a grateful and majestic Prague. The people welcomed their airmen home with flags and dancers on the streets.

Bozděch scanned the crowds for the familiar faces of his family whom he hoped would be there to meet him. But they were not in the crowd of well-wishers. Then, an officer of the Czechoslovak Inspectorate took the man and his dog to one side. In a side room, relatives told the airman that during the time he was in France and Britain his mother, his father and his uncle had been arrested and interrogated for three weeks by the Gestapo – they were punished for having a son who was fighting for the Allies. His mother and uncle were released but not his father. Transferred to an internment camp in Moravia his father was eventually released on the advice of the camp medic although the physical and psychological damage had already been done. He would never be the same again. Bozděch was shocked by the news and just wanted to get home to see his family.

After receiving his legal release papers, Bozděch was able to take Antis home to Soběkury where he saw his parents for the first time in six years. It was an emotional reunion but anger overwhelmed Bozděch's sadness. Looking at his parents and seeing how the years in the hands of the Gestapo had aged them and how it had taken its toll on their health, fury welled up inside him. They had suffered because of his actions and he felt a deep sense of guilt that he was to battle with for the rest of his life. And what about Antis, the new member of the family? Everyone was so pleased to meet the dog the world had written about. Since their historic return to Prague, the newspapers had started to swell with stories of the airman and the mascot dog of No. 311 Squadron. Everyone wanted to meet Antis and to write about him and that pleased Bozděch very much.

For Bozděch, one of the greatest pleasures of being home was being able to walk in the woods, just as he had done as a boy, and show Antis all the places that were special to him. He now had three weeks' leave before taking up a position with Transport Command in preparation for the launch of Czechoslovak Airlines. This time there was no problem with having a dog along for company – well, not this particular dog anyway – he was now the proud holder of a permit issued by Air Vice Marshall Janoušek himself. Antis was now a military dog. Certainly, he had served his time in three Air Forces and would do it all again if his health could have survived it. Reluctantly, Antis had to sit out his master's frequent flights to various European destinations but he was no longer upset about being left behind; he knew now that Bozděch would never leave him.

The autumn of 1945 was a rollercoaster of a time for Antis and his master who was enjoying every second of being back in his homeland. He had not only gained the rank of captain but also a new job as technical advisor to the Czechoslovak Air Force which put him in a very influential position with the Ministry of Defence. Just two months after meeting the girl who steeped out of the crowd and kissed this returning exile at Ruzyn Airfield, Bozděch married her in front of both families and as many friends as he could gather for the celebration in February 1946. Her name was Tatiana Zilka. Antis, of course, was there and stealing the show whenever possible. He was not allowed into the church ceremony but he more than made up for being denied that honour by dominating the photo session and getting himself tangled in the bride's long veil and train. Everyone laughed as the happy couple made way for Antis to be included in the wedding photographs and Tatiana's smile showed that she too had accepted her husband's dog as an integral part of their relationship.

Antis would continue to be an important part of Bozděch's peacetime life. All three moved in to a beautiful and spacious flat close to the Vlatava River in Prague. It was a wedding gift from the airman's old friend and now Minister of Foreign Affairs, Dr Jan Masaryk. The two had become great friends when Masaryk visited No. 311 Squadron on various bases. Antis recognized Masaryk too and made a point of jutting his moist German Shepherd muzzle into the minister's hands. Tatiana's father, an army colonel, had been high profile during the Prague Rising in May of that year so everyone in the family was familiar with the need to continue the fight for democracy, if and when required. For now, Bozděch was happy to leave politics to one side: if that was at all possible in his country.

Life was good for him and for Antis too. For the first time since meeting Bozděch, the dog was able to enjoy life away from airbases. And he discovered that it had certain freedoms and luxuries that he had never known before. Walks that were not accompanied by shelling or the sound of distant gunfire. Rest that was not broken by sirens or explosions. And he no longer had to miss his master when he went away on sorties. Antis was loving every minute of peacetime. As for his master, he was enjoying his job and having the time to indulge one of his greatest loves: writing. His most famous book (he penned four in total) was called *Gentlemen of the Dusk,* and it followed the crews of No. 311 Squadron on their perilous night bombing raids. He wrote it as a tribute to the men he flew with in Bomber Command who dedicated their lives to their country flying the mighty Wellington bombers. In order to write his books, Bozděch was given special access to official documentation and personal papers. He knew this access, some of which was arranged via the British Attaché in Prague, put him in a privileged position but he had no idea that, in twelve months' time, it would put him and his family in extreme danger.

Life became even better in July 1947 with the birth of a baby son, Jan. Antis adored the new arrival and watched over him as if it was his job to protect the baby from everyone else. Their old family friend, Dr Jan Masaryk, was the boy's godfather and namesake and Jan's christening, which took place in a church in Prague, was attended by guests of all social classes. To an outsider it must have looked as if democracy was living and breathing in Czechoslovakia. Unfortunately, that was not the reality at all.

On 10 March 1948, Dr Jan Masaryk, Minister for Foreign Affairs, was found dead in the courtyard of the Ministry. Slowly but surely, the Communist Party had infiltrated many of the top government jobs and now the body of democracy and all that Masaryk, Bozděch, their families and friends had fought for was beginning to weaken. The country was falling under the Soviet spell and democrats were forced to seriously consider their position: should they stay and wait to be told to leave, or just leave? For men like Bozděch and his fellow airmen, the situation was potentially far worse. They had flown with the French Air Force and the British RAF during the war, and this behaviour was regarded as unacceptable. Bozděch's books and articles about his wartime exploits and the contacts he quoted and referred to, placed him under suspicion. Just three days before he died, Masaryk had told his friend that their names were on a 'Red purge list'. No one believed the reports that Masaryk committed suicide. Everyone knew he had been murdered.

It had been just under three years since Bozděch returned home a hero and now he had to leave a fugitive. It was clear to his family and friends that he would have to flee but he could not tell his wife when he was leaving. As long as she was ignorant of her husband's whereabouts she would be safe. If he stayed they would all be in danger. All he could promise was that once settled in Britain he would make sure she and their son, Jan, followed him. But there was someone he could take with him – Antis. The day he left was going to look like any ordinary day at work, with Antis, the war dog, beside him. They left the office to attend a meeting and did not return.

There were two others taking the same route south-west from Prague but not everyone agreed that taking a dog was the best idea. Bozděch told them he 'trusted the dog to smell out danger long before you or I could hear or see it' and that they either travelled with him and the dog or they travelled alone. They had no choice but to agree. After a series of journeys which took them safely out of Prague, they approached the border on foot. They took one last look at their ancient and beautiful city, but they could not afford to stop. Now it was down to survival and it would not be long before the countryside would be crawling with guards. The terrain ahead of them was a mixture of dense wood and open pasture which they had to navigate before finding a safe place to lie low until dusk arrived to give them cover. Bozděch had Antis walk to heel in the wooded area and then sent him ahead as the forward scout to sniff out the pasture land. He had been well-trained for this and when the dog returned, the men knew it was safe to walk ahead. Antis was already proving an invaluable companion.

Waiting for dusk seemed to take forever and the travellers were already cold and fearful of what lay ahead. Bozděch's thoughts drifted to what he had left behind: his wife and child and his family who were so precious to him. He thought how Tatiana would have realized something was afoot when she discovered Antis gone from the flat and her suspicions would have been confirmed when her husband did not return from work. They had discussed the need for him to leave and agreed it was for the best for his family. She knew that it would happen one day soon but not knowing if he was alive or dead was bound to hurt. If their plan was working Tatiana would be on the way to her parents' home with Jan before she was removed by force from their beautiful flat. He prayed his little family was safe and would remain so until they could all be together once more. They were certainly safer with him gone. And his wife would be pleased to know that Antis was there protecting him as he had done so many times before.

As dusk fell, Antis began to act more and more like a wild animal: all his senses were heightened to take in everything around him, every smell that lingered in the air, the taste of the dewy grass around them. He lay at his master's side, waiting. As darkness eased through the dusk, the men prepared to leave their hiding place. An open field lay ahead of them and Antis took up position by his master's side. Suddenly, the dog hit the ground. Had he picked up a smell or the sight of something in the distance? Bozděch grabbed the dog's collar. He could feel the tension in his body. There was something out there ahead of them. They decided to lie low. Then the night's silence was broken by a group of people moving through the long grass beside them. Then searchlights beamed in and machine-gun fire lit up the sky. Border guards with trucks and tracker dogs teamed all over the area. They were hunting another group of escapees. Bozděch and the other men kept low and quiet, hoping they wouldn't be spotted, as the guards checked that the escapees had been dispatched and then disappeared. Antis rested his muzzle on his master's hand. It was safe to move on.

Eventually, they reached the river. Desperate to find a safe place to cross in the darkness, they stumbled into the water. Bozděch held Antis's collar tightly and they moved forward together. The water was cold and the current made it difficult to keep a sure footing. As the three men made the crossing, they drifted apart. When Antis pulled his master ashore they found they were alone. Bozděch knelt down to his dog and whispered the word, 'Seek'. Immediately, the dog re-entered the water and moments later he returned with one of the men clinging to his collar. He was much longer searching for the third man but finally he brought him out – he had been swept downriver.

The dog and the men were exhausted but they still had a long way to go. They pressed on through more woods and then climbed up a steep mountain where they were stranded on the hillside overnight, the cold chilling them through their wet clothes. Antis had done well to keep everyone together and Bozděch stroked his dog's head and held him close to thank him for his loyalty. The warmth from the dog's body gave the airman an idea: each of the men should hug Antis to keep themselves and the dog alive overnight. It was a valuable survival technique and everyone made it to the morning.

The border was close now. Antis may have been tired but all his senses were alert. It was unusual to hear him growl and so when he did the men took notice. Out of the morning mist the three men caught sight of Antis standing up ahead, his four legs splayed out on the chest of a border patrol guard. Never had Bozděch seen his dog be so aggressive; it was as if he knew that to let this man go would put the entire mission in jeopardy. They could not be sure that even if the guard was Czechoslovak he would allow them to walk over the border so, to be safe, they bound and gagged him and tied him to a tree then started their descent of the hillside. It was a relief to see the bend in the river ahead of them and the line of stones marking the border into Germany just beyond that. It wasn't clear if the small wooden hut close by was occupied or not but Antis went to find out by scratching at the door – it was empty. With no one to threaten them, the three men and one dog were free to wade in the river and run up its bank to freedom.

Antis was unaware of the significance of their journey but Bozděch could see that he was stressed and, for the first time in his life, anxious of humans. This was not how it should be and it was clear the dog was in need of peace and something close to normality. His master was in need of the same.

They had crossed the border into the American Zone of Occupation where the men were required to hand in their service revolvers and complete various formalities – they were now officially refugees – before being taken by Jeep to the US Air Force base at Straubing. There they met other escaped Czechoslovak airmen some of whom Bozděch had served with in the past. The men were grateful for the opportunity to talk to other men in the same situation, men who understood the emotion of their situation. Everyone shared one concern and that was for the welfare of their families left behind. Bozděch heard that Tatiana had left Prague with their son and gone to her parents' home as he hoped she would. At least he knew they were safe.

Now he had to secure his position and decided he must rejoin the RAF. Others were doing the same and the British Air Ministry was quick to recognize the value of these men to the peacetime Air Force. The enlistment procedures for ex-RAF personnel who had served in the war was relaxed to allow the Czechoslovakians to be absorbed back into the Service. All they had to do was wait for their visas as naturalized British citizens to be approved. This period of waiting took its toll on Antis and the holding camp at Regensburg was a trauma too far for the usually happy dog. He refused to eat the dog food that had been smuggled in for him and in desperation Bozděch started to force-feed his dog with a spoon. Both hated the experience and the indignity was overwhelming. There was only one thing Antis enjoyed about this time in his life and that was his walks and the chance to swim in the Danube. At least this was a hint of better things to come.

Antis and Bozděch escaped Prague on 27 April 1948 and it was 4 July before the British Air Ministry transported the Czechoslovak recruits to officially enlist at the RAF Headquarters in Wiesbaden. They were then taken on to Frankfurt to pick up their passports from the British Embassy. It was here that Bozděch was told that his dog would have to stay behind as he would not be allowed into Britain. This was totally unexpected. How could he leave without Antis? The dog had saved his life a thousand times over. He was his companion, his friend, his last link with his wife and family in his homeland. Antis was the only reality in a surreal world. He could not bear this.

Bozděch had spent the past weeks travelling between the holding camps trying to secure safe passage and the promise of a visa for his wife and son so they could join him. During that time, he travelled through many of the German towns he had been instrumental in bombing as part of No. 311 Squadron. He saw the devastation of the buildings and the infrastructure of enemy's homeland. He saw the people, stripped of their homes and running scared. He knew how that felt. He was a refugee too. He had fled his home in fear and all that separated him from desolation and hopelessness was the loyalty of one companion – Antis. Bozděch refused to travel without his dog. He appealed to the RAF and the Air Ministry – he knew that ultimately he must accept the decision that was to come from the top. Bozděch suddenly realized the extent of his dog's fame and importance within the Service. Antis was listed as an RAF war dog and so his owner's request was treated with the utmost sensitivity and seriousness. It was put to Bozděch that he would leave ahead of Antis who would remain in the care of a Corporal Hughes while the dog's documentation was prepared for travel to Britain. The process was likely to take several weeks and, while they appreciated this was not ideal, it was the only way Antis could travel within the regulations.

Bozděch was relieved at the offer and he was allowed to inspect the Corporal's quarters and the bunk where Antis would be sleeping. He was about to trust a perfect stranger with the life of his greatest friend and this did not come easily for a man who had been separated from everything else he held dear. But there was something about Hughes that Bozděch liked and respected. He was a serviceman too and with that came an indestructible loyalty to his fellow airman. He had faith in the man that he would care for his dog. Antis warmed to the man too and that was enough to convince the Czechoslovak that everything was as right as it could be in these impossible circumstances.

Bozděch stayed with Antis in Hughes's quarters until it was time for him to board the overnight crossing from the Hague to Harwich. The airman held Antis close to him and, speaking in hushed tones, just as he had done when Antis was a puppy fleeing France inside his master's flying jacket, he told the dog to behave and remember they would be together again very soon. He stroked the dog's glossy, sable-coloured head and walked away.

Within days of arriving at RAF Cardington in Bedford, Bozděch received a letter from Corporal Hughes reassuring the airman that his dog was well and only pining a little. Two weeks later, Antis arrived in Britain and was taken immediately to the quarantine kennels in Hackbridge in Surrey. The Air Ministry had stayed true to their word and had also arranged a pass for Bozděch to visit his dog. Antis sensed his master before he even came into view. By the time he reached the kennel, Antis was virtually leaping in the air with excitement. He looked healthy and happy which was a testament to Corporal Hughes's great care and a huge relief for Bozděch. Man and dog stayed together all day, walking and playing as they used to do. They had never been apart so long before and both had found it traumatic.

When they parted that first evening, Bozděch held Antis's head in his hands and explained that he had to leave him now but that he would be back to visit all the time. It was as if the dog understood every word – maybe he did. In his usual stoic way, Antis put his muzzle on his master's hand as if to say, 'It's fine ... I understand,' before allowing his master to walk away. Every Wednesday and Saturday, Bozděch visited Antis in the kennels and they would spend hours walking, talking and playing together just like the old times. Antis would always be sitting bolt upright waiting for his master to appear. He had the look of an airman standing to attention but there was a certain sadness to his face which was due, in part, to the way his left ear was now permanently bent over. The splinter of shrapnel that embedded itself when the Wellington bomber, Cecilia, was attacked by enemy fighters would forever be a reminder that this dog was a war hero, injured in conflict.

Just when it looked as if man and dog were entering a period of relative peace and security, Bozděch injured his leg in a sporting accident and was refused permission to travel from the rehabilitation hospital in Plymouth to Hackbridge. When the kennel visits stopped, Antis's health went into decline. At first when his master didn't show, Antis tried to escape to find him. Then he refused to eat. But it was the look he developed that told staff the dog was giving up the fight for life. They had to contact Bozděch and get the airman there before it was too late. Had his dog been almost any other dog, Bozděch would have been separated from him long before but it was the publicity surrounding Antis's service with Bomber Command and the many newspaper articles that covered his courage and loyalty that saved him. He was a hero and his famous bravery was admired by everyone who met him. Within twenty-four hours, Bozděch had been transferred to a rehab centre in Surrey and he was on his way to Antis's side.

Nothing could have prepared the airman for the sight that met his eyes. The dog was too weak to even raise his head in response to his master's voice. Despite the pain in his leg, Bozděch knelt down at his dog's side and took his head in his hands. He spoke to him gently, urging him to eat and then just sat stroking the dog's lean body to comfort and reassure him. Antis looked up at his master and through the sadness he expressed what his owner took as forgiveness. They remained like that for hours, though Bozděch knew that he would have to leave all too soon. And when that time came, Antis started to tremble and fear crept back into his face. The airman remembered a trick that had worked in the past to reassure his dog that he would return – he left his gloves by Antis's pillow.

The vet's prognosis was grim. There was nothing he could do medically for the dog. It was now down to his spirit and his will to live. Life had never seemed more in the balance than it did at that moment. For Bozděch, the vet's words told him only one thing: he was about to lose another part of his life, of himself, of his past and his future. Instead of catching the bus back to the hospital, he wandered into a church, and, as he wrote later, 'spoke to his God in the fullness of his heart' (*Freedom in the Air,* Hamish Ross). The next morning a call came in from Hackbridge asking him to visit. Bozděch prepared for the worst. But there, right in front of him, barking huskily, was Antis. It was a miracle turn of events: the dog had started to eat and he had shed the lost look in his eyes. Every day, his owner visited and he could see the gradual improvement in Antis's condition and temperament. He wanted to live again, this time knowing with absolute surety that his master would always come back for him, no matter what.

When Antis emerged from quarantine in January 1949, the bill for kennelling was way beyond Bozděch's means, totalling twenty-five shillings a week over six months. Bozděch applied to British charity PDSA (then known as the People's Dispensary for Sick Animals) for financial assistance. He was desperate – he had never asked anyone for anything before but he could not give up on the dog now. Once again, the high profile of the war dog paid off and the charity agreed to assist with the costs. And there was another reason for the help: PDSA had a nomination for Antis to receive a PDSA Dickin Medal, the award internationally recognized as the animals' Victoria Cross. The Air Ministry and the War Office provided proof that this dog was deserving of the highest honour for an animal in conflict. At the presentation of the medal at Earl's Court in London on 14 March 1949, the guests, including Field Marshall, the Earl Wavell, hero of the North Africa Campaign (who brought his granddaughter to meet the famous Antis), heard how Antis had been a constant and loyal companion to his owner and to the crew of the Wellington bomber of No. 311 Squadron. They heard how his company had supported them during the night raids and his courage under fire had inspired them. Bozděch, as always, took a back seat when Antis was in the limelight but he was filled with pride and admiration for the hero dog he had once carried close to his chest in the warmth of his flying jacket.

Antis was the first dog from overseas to be awarded the large bronze medal and in his speech, Field Marshall, the Earl Wavell, referred to the qualities of his Czechoslovak upbringing: 'This award ... you have worthily earned by the steadfastness, endurance and intelligence for which your race is well known. You have been your master's guardian and saviour. I am sure everyone will join me in congratulating you on your award, and we wish you many years in which to wear it.' (*One Man and His Dog*, Anthony Richardson).

For a dog that had endured so much, he deserved some peace and for the next four years he was able to enjoy life in a place he loved best – in earshot of aircraft. For the last two years of his life, Antis accompanied Bozděch on a posting to RAF Dalcross on the south shore of the Moray Firth in Scotland. The wild country-side reminded Bozděch of Bohemia and it was only a short journey from RAF Evanton where the pair had spent so many of the war years. One afternoon, they decided to visit the now-deserted airfield to take a look around the buildings that conjured up so many memories for them both. Bozděch was to write of this moment much later as if he was an observer saying: 'It seemed to the man that time had stood still in this place while only he and Antis had changed. To satisfy the dog, Jan pushed open the creaking outer door of the hut. In a moment Antis stood before their old room, on the door of which the scratch marks of his paws showed clearly despite the passage of time.'

The deserted airfield and its ghostly huts and towers were a stark realization that man and dog were the ones who had changed more than any of the places they once knew. He knew there was another change ahead and it was one he could not bare to think about. Already, he had been forced to accept that he would never see his family in Czechoslovakia again and to have to say goodbye to Antis would compound the profound and painful sense of loss.

They spent Christmas on the base and took advantage of the wintry landscape for some short but bracing walks. But it was clear to Bozděch that Antis was finding walking more and more difficult and it was not the pleasure it used to be. One night, as Antis rested his head on his master's chest, the dog's weight fell heavily. When asked to jump down, he delayed and then, stumbling, he collapsed. He received heat treatment twice a day in the sick bay but deterioration was starting to show in other areas. His sight and hearing were diminishing and his appetite declined. He moved like a dog in pain although he would still wait all day in the outdoors for his master to return from his duties. That was a habit too hard to break.

By the summer the dog was visibly ill and Bozděch was well aware that the hardest decision he would ever have to make for his companion was very close. One warm August evening, Antis and the airman were out on a short walk together. Only the airman knew it would be their last. The next morning they took a train from Inverness to London and then out to the PDSA sanatorium in Ilford, Essex. Bozděch had spoken to his friends at PDSA some weeks earlier and, according to his personal writings, one of the charity's veterinary surgeons had sent a telegram in response: 'Advise putting old friend out of misery. Grave reserved.'

Arriving at the sanatorium, Bozděch caught that now familiar glance from Antis that said, 'Don't worry … Everything is fine.' As Antis was placed on the consulting table, Bozděch lay his head next to his faithful dog and for the last time spoke soft and calming words of encouragement and thanks. Antis nuzzled his head into the hands that stroked his face and then suddenly opened his eyes, searching for his master's tear-sodden face. The moment was brief but that last connection was made as the war dog's body let go its last breath.

Antis was fourteen years old when he died. The grave the PDSA had prepared for him was in the charity's animal cemetery in Ilford where other dogs who had been awarded the PDSA Dickin Medal for bravery in World War Two were also laid to rest. The grave of this Czechoslovak war dog is made of granite and stands head and shoulders above the smaller memorials as befits the final resting place of a hero. Beneath the poem of hope inscribed on the white stone there is an inscription in Czechoslovak which reads: *VĚRNÝ AŽ DO SMRTI* – loyal unto death.

Taking Antis's collar with him, Bozděch returned to his posting in Scotland and began a period of grief that was to last his lifetime. In later life he reconnected with

his love of nature taking many walks. He would sometimes record the dawn chorus though he would never
play it back – maybe he just wanted to capture something
pure and precious.

He often met people who wanted to talk over the old
times and reminisce about the days with Antis and
Bomber Command but Bozděch could not bring himself
to revisit the past – it was too painful. The loss of Antis
was the loss of the bridge that linked the old and the new.
The loss of the silent friend who never judged the man
for anything he did or did not do. He accepted the man
for exactly who he was: a man of quiet dignity and bold
integrity. Like the dog he loved so dearly, he gave loyalty
beyond measure. And when he said, 'I will never have
another dog', it was with a loyalty that went beyond
death.

Tangye –

Fearless
Under Fire

'"I am serving in Afghanistan and have befriended a young stray dog that lives in the military base where I am stationed. Can you please help me rescue it? I just can't leave it here to starve."

'I smiled as I read the email. I needed to reply quickly. I knew that the soldier would want to know there was somebody else in the world who thought like he did. I had another dog to rescue.'

(Pen Farthing – ex-Royal Marine Commando and founder of the charity NOWZAD, which is dedicated to rescuing animals like Tangye in war-torn Afghanistan. *One Dog at a Time*, Ebury Press.)

Tangye was a tiny bundle of dusty black fur when Rik Groves of 29 Commando, Royal Artillery first set eyes on him. The puppy was lying on the floor at the feet of an Afghan security guard whose huge boots dwarfed the scrap of a dog. Maybe it was the unfamiliar sound of the English accent that interested him enough to raise his head out of the hot dirt but it was a chance for the soldier to catch a glimpse of what looked like a Labrador's face. No more than five or six weeks old, he was too young to be without his mother and maybe that explained why he was never more than a paw's pace from the yellowish, Corgi-type dog that was strutting around him. That dog looked streetwise but the pup's sad and innocent expression bothered the soldier and, unable to resist any longer, he reached down to stroke its bony body. That first touch was the start of a four year friendship that was to brighten the days and hearten the morale of British soldiers stationed in one of the most dangerous places on earth.

Kajaki lies on the Helmand River approximately 160 kilometres north of Camp Bastion and 100 kilometres northeast of Helmand Province's capital, Lashkar Gāh. The only way to reach the mountainous Kajaki by road is to take Highway 611 which winds through the Taliban-infested desert and patches of scrubland that typify the area. The road is a recognized hotspot for insurgent activity and troops taking this long and perilous road face the ever-present dangers of being ambushed and falling victim to IEDs (Improvised Explosive Devices) designed to cause maximum harm to anyone in their path. At the heart of this stark desert base shimmer the turquoise waters of the Kajaki Dam. The vast pool is the only visible respite from the blinding dazzle of the white sand. In summer, with temperatures reaching around 50°C and in winter falling to a little as –25°C, it is a desperately inhospitable place to live at any time of year. The rains which come between October and April provide little respite from the extremes as they only turn the sand into deep, clinging, yellow mud. The contrast between the heat of the day and the cold nights can deceive the newcomer and prove a harsh reality for stray dogs that roam the area.

Dogs found wandering in Afghan communities are no longer adopted as pets. Since the arrival of the Taliban, dogs are considered to be dirty and are treated with disdain; they are commonly shunned and often abused and tortured. It is not unusual to see a puppy used as a football in the street or kept lean and mean to fight for money. The harsh reality for many dogs in Afghanistan is that if he is not a good fighter his life will not be worth living and it will be painfully short. Luckily, little Tangye did not have the telltale signs of a dog being groomed for fighting. For a start, he still had his ears and tail intact. And, looking at the skinny bag of bones that he was, it was unlikely Tangye would develop the necessary physique to be a prize fighter. In that respect, Tangye was maybe one of the lucky ones: too skinny to be a fighter, too small to be a threat but attractive enough to be adopted by the guards stationed at the Kajaki Dam militia post. Tethered to a stake, given no food and no water. Just there. That was Tangye.

Warrant Officer Rik Groves was heading up the first Operations Mentoring Liaison Team (OMLT) the British Army had raised in the Kajaki area since the Taliban poured out of the religious schools and refugee camps of Pakistan and Kandahar twelve years before. His right-hand man was Sergeant Lee Mildener of 45 Commando, Royal Marines and, to help them both communicate with the local people, an interpreter went along too. In charge of ten or so Afghan National Army (ANA) soldiers, this was an embryonic force created to establish a good working and living relationship with the local people, most importantly the local tribesmen and elders who hold sway in their communities. These people had lived and thrived quite happily on their land and prospered by farming cereal and growing fruit and continuing a culture that embraced the rituals of an ancient people. The terrorist attack on New York's World Trade Center on 11 September 2001 changed all of that. Terrorism had raised its ugly head in the spotlight of the world and the war against its leader, Osama bin Laden, all associated with him and those protecting him was declared by the United States and backed by the British Government.

On 7 October 2001, two British hunter-killer submarines entered the Arabian Sea off the coast of Pakistan. Nuclear ships *HMS Trafalgar* and *HMS Triumph* launched a hail of Tomahawk cruise missiles. The 455-kilogramme guided missiles destroyed a Taliban training school in the Afghan countryside. It was the start of a targeted aerial bombing campaign that gave the overthrown Afghan Northern Alliance the power to return fire on their attacker, the Taliban. Under the direction of their warlord general, Rashid Dostum, and backed by the US Special Forces, the Alliance retook the holy city of Mazar-i-Sharif and powered south to regain Kabul. That was on 21 November 2001, the same day the Alliance also took control of Bagram airbase, a strategically vital move.

What followed was two years of consolidation for the Afghan National Alliance with the support of the British and US Forces. The thrust of each military operation was to secure the position of the Alliance against the Taliban and capture the insurgents, giving them little time or space to retreat to their stronghold over the Pakistan border. By the time the US and British Governments began to turn their attention to the activities in Iraq in 2003, the position in Afghanistan was favourable to the Alliance.

Although the Alliance may not have agreed with the way the military operations had been performed, the result was conclusive: four days after the Alliance had retaken Bagram airbase, a C-130 Hercules had landed 100 elite British Commandos from the Special Boat Service (SBS). Living their motto 'By Strength and Guile' to the last letter, the men secured the base and set up effective air traffic control. In securing the base and adopting it as headquarters for the British Special Forces, the area became as safe as it could be, especially with the imminent arrival of 120 men (two squadrons) of Special Air Service (SAS) personnel in readiness for an attack deep into enemy territory. The successful destruction of an al-Qaeda opium storage plant, in broad daylight, earned the regiment a Distinguished Service Order, two Conspicuous Gallantry Crosses and two Military Crosses. They proved absolutely their motto – 'Who Dares Wins'. Commandos from the SBS were getting close to bin Laden in December 2001 when the US Forces infiltrated the Tora Bora cave system close to the Khyber Pass. With the help of the SBS, US Forces were guided into position and successful air strikes crippled al-Qaeda insurgents, forcing them into a rearguard action. Countless enemy positions were located, attacked and cleared but this was guerilla warfare and it was being fought close to the enemy's main retreat in Pakistan where they were always bound to run.

Lives were lost but the result was clear – the enemy was on the run. Between 2003 and 2005, British Forces in Afghanistan fell to just 300 and under the umbrella of Nato's International Security Assistance Force (ISAF) the troops supported the Afghan National Alliance from their base in Kabul. Meanwhile, as the US and British Forces turned their attention to Iraq, the Taliban used this breathing space to their advantage. They regrouped and re-equipped themselves for war.

Spring 2006, Operation Herrick IV: over 3,000 soldiers of the 16 Air Assault Brigade arrived in Helmand. They were to launch a reconstruction project in southern Afghanistan using the capital of Helmand Province, Lashkar Gah, as the centre of its operations. Devised to bring prosperity to the local people and their environment, the plan would also win support away from the Taliban and weaken their hold on Helmand. The British Government hoped this could be achieved in peace and without an exchange of gunfire. But the politicians had underestimated the feeling on the ground and the arrival of the British troops was not going to be a confirmation of peace and rebirth after all. When the Afghan President, Hamid Karzai, requested the British Commanders take their men out of the capital and position them close to the Taliban strongholds in the mountains of the north, it was the start of the domino effect that took the soldiers into direct combat with the enemy.

Three British regiments had arrived with the mission to keep peace and increase prosperity and soon found themselves defending their positions and their lives. The troops from the 1st Battalion, The Royal Irish Regiment, the 2nd Battalion, The Royal Gurkha Rifles and 3 Para were posted to platoon houses in Musa Qaleh, Now Zad and Sangin. And within days they were involved in unexpected combat. In June 2006, the British lost their first soldier in combat with the Taliban. He was shot dead when the Quick Reaction Force (QRF) was ambushed on its way to save a patrol being pinned down by the enemy. In August, A Company, 3 Para lost twenty-nine-year-old Bryan Budd. Corporal Budd was leading a patrol protecting engineers working on the platoon house in Sangin. His patrol outmanoeuvred a group of Taliban fighters who were spotted coming through a cornfield towards the house. Budd disposed of two Taliban fighters before his life was taken in the crossfire. He was awarded a posthumous Victoria Cross. By 2 September, the British Forces had lost another fourteen lives as an RAF Nimrod surveillance aircraft crashed into the desert taking with it the hopes of turning Operation Herrick IV into a peaceful tour of duty.

When Rick Groves landed in Helmand Province on 17 September 2006, he was confused as to how the troops could have been sent out to blend in and build relationships with local people when the Taliban were still as potent a force as they were in 2001. The Taliban had banned music and dancing and prohibited women from any kind of public life. They had introduced rules that had set the development of their own society back hundreds of years. Closing schools, shooting teachers and imposing gender rules created an atmosphere of fear and stagnancy for the ordinary people whose lives and fortunes had been changed so dramatically in the Taliban takeover. British and US Forces had given the insurgents a military thrashing but the organization was not the toothless tiger it was perceived to be by the West. Fanatics who aim to kill do not hand over their hard-won territory to Nato's ISAF or anyone else. But if the people could see the British soldiers were there now to protect them and improve their status and environment following over a decade of hardline Taliban rule then the work could begin on making Kajaki a better place to live. The Nato ISAF forces remained determined to restore what had been damaged but it all had to be done under the watchful eye of the Taliban. For the Western soldiers brought in to start the transformation, this still looked like a war of justice versus terrorism.

The morning Rik and Lee first set eyes on Tangye they were on a routine visit to the security post at the dam. Both men had arrived in Afghanistan just days before and this dog was the first thing they had encountered that reminded them of home in the UK. They called him Tangye, after a local village. It just seemed to suit him. Having been dog owners for most of their lives, it was no wonder this vulnerable Labrador fired an instinct to protect and care for this voiceless victim of the war.

When Rik and Lee arrived in Kajaki in September 2006, it was a remote northern outpost with few home comforts and even fewer people. Nestled in this mountainous region sits the Kajaki Dam and its vitally important hydro-electric power station which provides electricity to Helmand and parts of Kandahar. To the British Forces, the Kajaki Dam is a huge asset to the area and capable of supplying electricity to many more homes. With electricity comes communication and a way to inform the local people of the relative stability that existed in some areas. This is not something the Taliban wants anyone to hear and so the dam is an excuse to intimidate the dam workers and the local Afghan community. And, after each attack, the insurgents can retreat north to their safe havens. The troops went out on daily patrols both on foot and using the Jackal armoured vehicles (which also have a platform for heavy machine guns) in order to keep the enemy pushed back. This stark and dangerous area is ripe for the work of the OMLT and each time they visited, there was Tangye wearing his eager, friendly face.

It all began with a biscuit from the soldiers' ration packs. Tangye sat up and sniffed the air. The little velvet wrinkles on his forehead raised and lowered as he tried to place the smell. But he couldn't. It wasn't a smell he recognized and so he blew his nose, as dogs do, and shook his head to clear the confusion of his senses. But as Rik moved closer and the biscuit smell grew stronger, Tangye smacked his mouth and licked his lips in eager anticipation. Then, staying low, he crept up to the soldier to conduct an immediate body search using his dry, black muzzle to seek out the hidden biscuit.

'Ah, so that's what you want from me,' said Rik, staring down at the triumphant puppy who was now crunching loudly away on the biscuit he had tracked down to the soldier's pocket. Tangye frothed at the mouth as he savoured the biscuit and then its final crumbs, all carefully licked off the sand, turned to brown goo in the corner of his mouth. Rik had never seen a ration biscuit enjoyed so much. Everyone thought they were hard and tasteless but Tangye was already sniffing for more. 'So you want another one of those do you little guy? Well, we'll have to see what we can do on our next visit,' said

Rik, reaching out his hand to the timid puppy. It seemed Tangye wanted to be stroked but he wasn't sure how the process worked. Treats and affection were all new to him.

Visit after visit, Rik and Lee arrived with the intention of seeing Tangye and giving him plenty of fuss and the odd treat and it didn't take long for the puppy to get used to the attention. Within the space of two weeks, he went from being a shy and timid creature, almost too afraid to lift his head towards them, to becoming a bouncy, happy little dog around his new British friends. As soon as he saw Lee or Rik approach the gate, he would run to the full length of his tether to greet them and then launch his own sniffing ambush to seek out anything tasty they might have to offer. He never seemed to learn that running so fast with such a short length of rope around his neck was going to have the same painful result every time. Each time, it sprang back giving him a huge jolt to his neck. But every time he saw them he did the same thing, much to the soldiers' amusement. Just seeing him run, pink tongue lolling out of his mouth, his face so full of joy and enthusiasm, was amazing. Then to have him land rear end down in the dust was so typical of this character who, once he learnt how to enjoy himself, didn't know how to stop. It was obvious the dog was getting more and more attached to the two men and soon he was sitting, waiting for them to visit. He was no longer the sad, timid stray they first saw with his head in the dust. He was already so much more than that.

One day, as the men were walking away from Tangye's post, an idea was thrown into the conversation: 'Why don't we buy him?' The discussion between Rik, Lee, their interpreter and the medic was short and decisive. 'Good idea. I'll go and offer ten dollars,' announced Rik, quickly borrowing the money from the medic. With a little help from the interpreter, the negotiations for Tangye began. Lee was apprehensive. He was afraid the Afghans would realize how much the British wanted the dog and set the price too high but he need not have worried. The talks didn't last long. The security workers were amused by the idea that the soldiers wanted to pay good money for such a runt of a dog when they could pick up a much bigger stray from the desert for nothing. The ten dollars was readily accepted. The deal was done and the soldiers were on their way back to camp with their dog. Later, Rik wrote in his log: 'Tangye. Black Labrador. New Resident. 22 September 2006.'

Once back at camp, it was a matter of settling in the new recruit. The dog had only known a life of sleeping outdoors and most of that had been during the day. Sleeping through the intense heat is instinctive for dogs like Tangye, it is a coping mechanism which leads them to being more active at night. His new life with the soldiers was going to mean adjusting to sleeping indoors at night and that wasn't going to be an easy lesson, even for this young dog. There was only one way to do this and that was to start the first night the way they meant to go on. Putting paper on the floor and a blanket next to Rik's cot, the men settled Tangye in for his first night with the British in Afghanistan.

By morning, it was clear that Tangye was going to like living with people. Although he was restless in the night, he already knew that he could turn to either of his new friends for companionship and they would be there for him. He hadn't appeared to have a specific role at the Kajaki Dam security post – he was certainly way off fitting the criteria for being a ferocious guard dog as he wasn't big enough to scare people away or give chase to intruders if they breached the security gate. He was merely a dog on a rope and that was all. But those days were over for Tangye. Now he had a whole new set of friends and all he had to do was be himself. And what was most important to a dog waking to his first morning on camp was – breakfast. The soldiers' ration packs represented a vast new menu for the dog that was used to scavenging for every scrap of food. Selecting a boil-in-the-bag beef stew, Rik prepared and cooled it then offered it to Tangye who confirmed that it was an instant hit, even at breakfast.

The men were to learn the first lesson: a little food goes a long way when you're training a hungry dog. Even the limited offerings of the rations packs soon had Tangye eating out of their hands. A little of the meals mixed with army dog biscuits worked perfectly. It had taken a matter of two weeks to domesticate this almost feral dog and there was no way he was going to leave either them or his new home and all its comforts for a second. He was their dog now. And there was something very special about that relationship in an environment where war waged all around them.

The guys were determined that the dog would be well-behaved and socialized. He was sharing their camp space and there was really only room for a dog that would obey basic orders, at the very least. A private joke circulated that maybe Rik and Lee could train Tangye ahead of the Afghan National Army recruits, who were also learning the basics of military procedure and tactics. Taking the ANA recruits and Tangye under their wing were more than enough additional challenges in an environment where snipers, mortars and gunfire were part of the daily agenda. Certainly, the two men soon discovered that their sparky black puppy was eager to perform any task – as long as there was a meal at the end of it. Tangye had not seen much that impressed him in human nature so far. And that seemed a shame to them. After all, he was a Labrador and any Lab the men had encountered before had thrived on fuss and attention. Now Tangye had every chance of being the same. All he had to do was learn to trust the humans around him.

At the time Tangye joined the ranks of the British Army, the military base at Kajaki was in its early stages of development. The buildings had been the original summer retreat of the hierarchy in the Russian Army and last inhabited over thirty-five years before. Located on a high and beautiful spot, the rambling brick building offered showers and sleeping accommodation and even a swimming pool, although that had long stood empty on a site that had been battered and beaten over the years both inside and out. One group or another had inflicted deliberate physical damage in an effort to destroy it. But despite all of that, there was still an elegance to the walls that told of a grander past that would never have been tolerated by the Taliban.

From a military perspective, Kajaki was vulnerable as it did not have a Forward Operations Base (FOB), only the former United Nations base (now called Zeebrugge) patrolled by local Afghan security guards. But that didn't stop the base being a target for the Taliban. Within an hour of Rik Groves landing by helicopter in Kajaki on 18 September 2006, he was involved in a mortar attack. Rik had just about dropped his bags when the first mortar landed. A huge cloud of burnt dust filled the air. Blinded for seconds but hearing voices all around, Rik got his bearings and rallied into position. 'Move, move, move ...' the mortars hailed in as the soldiers' gunfire targeted the enemy position. A counter mortar team set-up: 'Fire!' A direct hit silenced the enemy attack. It was over with no military casualties. This would become an almost nightly occurrence for the men. And when Tangye was ready to join the ranks, he took the opportunity to show his new friends that he was not afraid to go into battle either.

At this time, 3 Para were still completing their tour of duty in Kajaki. They had suffered terribly as this had not been the tour they had been expecting. Peacekeeping had quickly turned to face-to-face combat with the Taliban and with fatal consequences. It was with 3 Para that Tangye chose to go on his first sortie. The mission was to last all day with Rik leading the OMLT and a group of ANA soldiers during the day with 3 Para going in under cover of night. That October morning Tangye sensed something was going to happen. He refused to settle and almost every hour Rik was stopped in his track by Tangye pressing his dewy nose into his face. He could feel the dog's body sway as his tail lashed from side to side, as much to say, 'Whatever it is you're up to, I'm coming with you.' It was no use Rik trying to comfort the dog. He had given up on that idea at about midday. Although he knew by now that an order to 'stay' from Rik or Lee meant just that, he also knew that this 'walk' was going to be different and the more excited he became the more determined he was to get in on the action.

The patrol was heading for a stretch of road north of the camp. It was a road well known to the insurgents who used a garage along it as a meeting place. It was suspected that they used the building for storing and sometimes launching their mortar attacks. The plan was to use the Afghan National Army as a diversion section and the others would take the road and place a sniper on the target building. The darkness providing a chance to capture the enemy, destroy a potential meeting place and hopefully commandeer a valuable cache of arms and explosives, depleting their stock and so temporarily reducing their military power.

As Rik and Lee talked all of this through with the interpreter, Tangye sat quietly at their feet. He seemed mesmerized by all that was going on. He was used to going out with his own pack of four men but the mass activity must have heightened his senses to feel this was something bigger.

Rik's instinct was to leave Tangye behind. He had no idea how the patrol would go and even less of an idea how the dog would behave if they met enemy fire. He was a two-month-old puppy and, although no stranger to gunfire, it had always been at a distance. Clearly, they would have to lock the dog away if he was staying behind but, left alone, the dog would bark and alert everyone, insurgents included, to the activities on the camp. The decision was finally taken: Tangye was going on patrol. It seemed the best option for everyone. Rik packed a bowl for water and a blanket for warmth. Kitted out and ready to move, the men gathered.

The soldiers prepared their kit for the night patrol. Night vision goggles became their most important piece of protection and the diversion party alongside them. There was an eerie quiet as the preparations reached completion. Every man in the patrol was aware that everywhere, day and night, was a perfect hiding place for a Taliban sniper or for an ambush. The soldiers moved in fear of the sniper's bullet. And it was wise to be so aware of the dangers as the Talibs know every contour of this land that the British soldiers were trying to protect. Taking a section of the Afghan National Army with them, the patrol moved out into the desert.

'Move out!' The patrol Commander gave the order and the men went forward. Tangye stayed close to his masters. This was not the usual walk, he knew that. But he was with Rik and Lee so he felt safe. They reached the first checkpoint. Tangye sat down. To Rik's surprise the dog had decided he was not going further. No one could take time to encourage him further, they had to move on. Tangye stayed behind. But would he be there when they returned? Moving on without Tangye was not easy for Rik or Lee. Although he had only been with them a short time he was their dog and to have to leave him in the desert like that was a big step. But a dog on patrol, unless he is a working dog, cannot be allowed to be a liability. Tangye was along for the walk and he had decided he did not want to walk any more. They had to leave him.

Heading back almost four hours after leaving Tangye, Rick and Lee felt apprehensive. If he was there, fine. But if he was not there and no immediate search of the area brought him out, they knew they would have to accept he had either been taken by the jackals or lifted by someone knowing he was a soldier's dog. If this was the case, he could have a price on his head that far exceeded the ten dollars that Rik had paid for him. As they approached the area where the dog had decided to stay put, the men could hear a muffled sound that was a mix of bark and whimper. Rik recognized it immediately – it was Tangye. He was sitting exactly where the patrol had left him four hours earlier. He had waited for the men to return and he greeted them like long-lost friends which, by now, of course, they were. Tangye had shown the men one important thing – he trusted them.

The operation moved on into the night and proved to be a success for the British. There was always a chance the Taliban would return to one of their lairs but for now, for that night, at least there was a victory for the British troops and no mortar attack on the base for the first time in many weeks. After that day the patrols would have to get used to a new sound, other than the crunch of soldiers' boots on stone breaking the eerie silence of the night. That was the hurried breathing of an eager black Labrador out for a long and hazardous walk.

A month later, in November 2006, Tangye had to say goodbye to his friends in 3 Para. The tour had not been the peacekeeping mission they had been promised and they had experienced losses and heavy casualties. It was now the turn of the Royal Marines of 3 Commando Brigade who, after the experience of 3 Para, were well aware that their operation, Herrick V, was to be one of attack. They were to engage the Taliban in constant fight-ing over the winter months. There was to be no let-up and no holding back on this military offensive. For Tangye, his day-to-day life would not change as his masters Rik Groves and Lee Mildener remained in Kajaki as the Operations Mentor Liaison Team now serv-ing alongside the Royal Marine Commandos. The British aim to restore the prosperity and cultural freedoms stolen by the Taliban in their takeover was still in opera-tion. This made the work of the OMLT more vital than ever. As for Tangye, he was about to make a name for himself.

His first experience of a military patrol had not put Tangye off his daily duties with the OMLT. As the team's constant companion, he was soon regarded as part of the outfit. The acceptance took a little more work with the local people who were suspicious of the black dog who followed the soldiers everywhere. They must have wondered why the soldiers would want to take a dog with them. After all, a dog is not the ideal companion in a society where dogs are considered dirty. If they were trying to impress, was this really the way to do it? Tangye had no idea that he wasn't welcome in certain places. It was part of Rik's job to visit the village elders and nurture a relationship with them that would transcend the military presence. These walkabouts were part of Tangye's daily routine and he bounded through each one with irrepressible enthusiasm. The elderly man who ran the local prison was happy to welcome the OMLT but Tangye was a different matter. Having this man on side was important to Rik and the team as the villagers often sought his opinion on a variety of matters. If he endorsed the military's plans then he would tell others to do the same and so draw attention and support away from the Taliban. At first, the man told the interpreter that he would not allow the dog beyond the garden but dining with the man and his daughter three or four times a week gave Rik a chance to show how well-behaved and funny Tangye was. Gradually, the dog was allowed closer and closer to the house and then, one day, he was let inside the house. In a society were dogs are regarded as the lowest of the low, this represented a huge respect for the soldiers and, by association, the dog too. As others saw this and word spread, it opened other doors to the OMLT too.

In the military camp in Kajaki, Tangye was welcomed by everyone. The ANA troops found the Western soldiers' relationship with him very strange at first but the more time they spent with the friendly Labrador, the more they warmed to the dog's personality. Even they were beginning to see that this wisp of a dog was bringing a certain comfort to everyone around him and bringing the gift of laughter to the camp. Even after an exhausting patrol, the sight of Tangye running around dragging someone's desert boot across the camp, the soldier frantically giving chase, was bound to raise a laugh. It was never a good idea to leave socks around as Tangye would choose the smelliest and take off with them. Being a sock thief was probably the worst of Tangye's vices, unless you count pinching food as a terrible crime. The British soldiers would often notice Tangye taking up position by the Afghan soldiers who set up small open fires to cook fish. Sleek and stealthy, Tangye would slide into position to move on the fish as soon as he had the smallest chance. He put his nose to the air as the fish was placed on the plates and then with a sudden rush and grab action the fish was gone! There was no way the hungry Afghans were going to catch the opportunist Labrador. Carrying no weight at all, the dog was gone before anyone could see more than a glimpse of his thin black legs and oddly bent tail disappearing in the distance. Now used to sharing food with his human friends, Tangye preferred to show off his 'catch' to Rik or Lee but often hunger got the better of him and so the most they saw of their dog's tasty prize was his crazy display of lip-licking!

Other camp dogs, and there were a few, learnt to steer clear of the local donkeys and the roaming camels – but not Tangye. It wasn't that he liked their company particularly, he just saw them as another prospective playmate. Biting at their heels, he was soon the centre of their attention and often he came off worse for it, almost always being on the receiving end of a nasty nip for his trouble. And while all this was happening, Tangye had an audience of soldiers to cheer him on. His antics were guaranteed to make them laugh and transport them away from the horrors of the conflict.

'Tangye was a natural comedian and brought laughter where there was little to laugh about,' said Rik Groves. 'We knew if Tangye was around, he would want comfort himself, looking for the soldier who needed comforting and his natural sense of mischief would always make us smile.'

Naturally, the soldiers could not help bringing things into camp that they knew would tease their crazy mascot dog. When Rik brought a singing Billy Bass fish into camp, he just knew that Tangye would either love or hate it – either way, the reaction would guarantee many smiles. The dog took one look at the fish's bendy body and talking head and barked uncontrollably. He looked at his friends and they were laughing too. 'It was as if he real-ized he had an audience and he was going to give them a show,' said Rik. 'There's no doubt Tangye knew laughter was a good thing and he did his best to make it happen as much as possible. That's what made his company so special. He was not held back by any army regulations or rules of engagement. He was a free spirit and we all loved and admired him for that. It was everything we could not be. He was the people's dog. Happy and free.'

The extremes of weather affected Tangye the same way they would the soldiers at home in the UK: he sought out a spot by the electric fire when it was cold and would lie there for as long as he could get away with. He would stay still even when the men tried to move him when they thought he just might singe his fur! In the heat it was tempting to cool this black dog down with the hose to make him more comfortable but Tangye would somehow manage to run in and bite at the water without getting wet. One time when on patrol, the route took them past a low point in the river with a slipway and Rik saw his opportunity to give Tangye his first swimming lesson. It was a good idea but once in the water, the dog did every-thing he could to get out as quickly as possible. It was so unusual for a Labrador to hate water – it just had to be a Tangye thing.

Army dog handlers would often come to Kajaki and, as Tangye was a friend to all dogs, he would always bounce up to introduce himself to the visitor. On one visit, the handler took the opportunity to remind Rik that it wasn't a good idea to make friends with the local dogs and that he was asking for trouble by taking on this once-feral dog. He recommended that Rik turned him out into the wild. Rik explained that the dog belonged to him and that he had paid for Tangye, trained him, socialized him and he was now used to the company of British soldiers and the taste of army rations. Besides, he was too valuable to the morale of the men to return him to the wild now. It would be cruel and it simply wasn't going to happen. Point taken, the dog handler backed off and simply showed his approval by leaving his supply of dog food behind for Tangye. Rik managed to arrange for Tangye to be vaccinated the next time the vet was on camp. As far as the men were concerned, this dog was to receive the best of care just like any well-loved pet back home. He was one of them and part of their team and always some-one to write home about.

Christmas 2006 was Tangye's first as the British soldiers' mascot in Kajaki and the dog's postbag was full of gifts from the friends and families of the men he was serving alongside. Since Tangye's arrival on the base, letters home had started to include news of the dog's antics and very soon the people back in the UK knew as much about the mascot as they did about their loved one – maybe more.

'The dog provides a distraction from the news of pain and suffering and fear,' says Lee Mildener. 'You don't want to worry your family more than they worry already, so for them to hear that there is something in that desolate place, so far from home, that brings comfort and laughter is good for everyone. Tangye was something good to focus on and everyone felt they knew him whether they were in Afghanistan or the UK. And if we were talking about Tangye then we weren't talking about the war.' Toys and treats arrived by the sackful for the stringy, black desert dog and it was up to Rik and Lee to make sure that he did not get too much of a good thing.

The letters, the treats, the recognition as army mascot all gave this adopted dog a sense of belonging. He was starting to spend more time with whoever was going out on patrol; additional military personnel were arriving and everyone wanted to meet the mascot dog they were hearing so much about. Although he never missed a patrol, Tangye would always return to Rik or Lee if he was scared or hurt. He still recognized them as his masters no matter who else came on the scene. The time he misjudged his clearance of a length of razor wire and gashed his stomach, he made his way to the two men who had adopted him for their comfort and help. And the medic patched him up making sure that the cut was clean and Tangye was fit to return to duty. Nothing less than the best of care was ever acceptable for their dog and identifying him as their dog became increasingly important too. Lee's wife, recognizing the importance of that dog to her husband, acquired a green camouflage collar and attached the Union flag and Tangye's name with OMLT underneath. No one wanted this special dog to get lost and not be able to find his way home. He was far too valuable a member of the team to risk that. He belonged to them and if he went anywhere, they wanted him back.

Owning a dog that was taken from the desert was not always going to be easy. The more secure and confident Tangye appeared to grow, the more of a free spirit he became. On the days his masters did not go on patrol, Tangye would go with whoever was heading out and it didn't matter where. The first time he stayed away overnight, he invited himself on a patrol into the mountains and by the time dusk arrived Tangye was nowhere to be seen. The last time anyone saw him he was bounding out of the camp gates leading the patrol, as was now his way, his tail and ears held high in anticipation of a good walk. 'You'd better behave yourself tonight Tangye,' was the request from the patrol leader. 'No barking and no giving the game away. Just be a good boy, right?' Tangye looked as if he understood the order to behave and everyone knew he would try his best. What they also knew was that if the Talibs were around, Tangye would sense their presence first. Always staying ahead but keeping close to the head of the group Tangye walked forward with stealth and with all five senses on alert. Suddenly he stopped, sat and put his nose to the air. 'Tangye's got something Sir,' This was a sign that could be ignored. Experience had taught the soldiers that much. 'What's he got Sergeant?' The night vision goggles didn't reveal anything but Tangye was determined the patrol should stay still. 'Stay where you are boys.' The patrol scanned the area. 'There's something out there, Sir.' Suddenly the patrol came under attack. Two stray insurgents had been surprised by the patrol and Tangye no doubt saved soldiers' lives that night. He got what he wanted and now he had an overnight stay in the mountains too.

'Is Tangye with you?' came the call on the radio from base.

'Affirmative,' came the reply. 'Tangye is here. He is fine. Will bring him back with us in the morning. Over.'

But he did not always plan his stays away quite so well. The time he went missing for ten days, the men were convinced he had been abducted. It was unlike him to be gone for so long and no one had seen him running with a patrol. Everyone was getting to know Tangye and it was becoming an unwritten rule that his position was radioed in to base if he was seen out and about. But this time there were no messages, no sightings and dwindling hope that he was going to make it back home. He had simply disappeared. It was by chance that Lee was on duty checking militia checkpoints and he noticed something he had not seen at one of the points earlier in the day. The door to the small outbuilding had been ajar but now it was closed and he picked up a muffled noise coming from inside. He insisted the Afghan militia guards opened the door. And when they did, there was Tangye tied up inside.

'That's our dog,' the interpreter said to the guards. 'That's our dog and we are taking him back.'

The guards decided not to challenge the soldiers. Maybe they thought there were better dogs to catch in the desert so why bother with this one. Whatever the reason, the door was opened and Tangye was taken off the rope. He was welcomed by a relieved Lee who had thought Tangye had gone for good. And back at base, Rik was there to say hello to the dog that almost got away. It was a miracle he still had his collar on. Happy as everyone was to have him back, no one wanted to speculate what was going to happen to the him next; it just didn't bear thinking about. The men had realized just how much they were becoming attached to the young Labrador. To have him there day after day and then suddenly nothing for ten days was quite a shock. Fears for their dog's safety had started to set in.

In March 2007, Warrant Officer Rik Groves and Sergeant Lee Mildener completed their tours of duty in Afghanistan. It was time to go home but someone very close to them had to stay. The men had grown to realize that, although they had bought the dog, the ten dollars they had paid did not really give them ownership of this dog. Tangye – named after a once thriving market town close to spot where he was first seen – belonged with whoever he could join on daily patrol or chasing camels, begging rations and stealing boots and socks. He had an entire desert to run in, if he wished, and more people to adore and admire him than many others have in a lifetime. With heavy hearts, both men completed their time and said their goodbyes to Tangye. And it was tough for Rik to look into those amber eyes and tell him to be a good dog. 'I could feel a lump in my throat. In the six months we shared with Tangye, he grew up before our eyes. Not just physically but in every other way too. He became confident enough to lead patrols from the front, meeting explosions head-on or from the top of a compound wall. He was unafraid and that was the quality that inspired the men. If a little dog could rise out of the dust and face the Taliban without fear then it was possible of anyone. And everyone believed that. He was no longer our dog. He was every soldier's dog.'

During the first six months of his military career, Tangye had seen the men he served with suffer some of the worst losses in the conflict in Afghanistan so far. The tour had seen many daring missions including the now legendary rescue mission at Jugroom Fort in Garmsir when two Apache helicopters with four volunteers strapped to their sides landed at the fort under heavy fire to rescue the body of a young Lance Corporal from Zulu Company of 45 Commando Royal Marines. These heroics won the rescuers two Distinguished Flying Crosses and three Military Crosses between them. Rik Groves had spent a week at Camp Bastion handling the repatriation of bodies being returned home. In one broken ceasefire, three men had been lost over just five days. The repatriation involved Afghan losses too. Each instance had a profound affect on the atmosphere and the mood in the camp. It was something every new arrival had to get used to and that included Tangye. He had made friends and lost them not knowing where they had gone. If dogs grieve then Tangye did it in his own way. And he helped those around him by bringing much needed laughter and comfort in equal measures.

Operation Herrick V had resulted in the creation of a three- to four-mile safety buffer around the dam. It was a layer of protection for the Labrador left behind. He was now going to experience the first of many handovers to subsequent OMLT personnel.

Running with other dogs – AK, Dopey, Gaydog – Tangye was always the leader of the pack. It was the same when he went on patrols with the men – they were also his 'pack'. Only Tangye was interested in joining the patrols. Gaydog ran away from the explosions (hence his not very politically correct name) just as quickly as Tangye ran towards them. He was unperturbed by the noise of the gunfire and the constant mortars. And he seemed oblivious to the danger he was in during an exchange of gunfire. He became so familiar with the sounds of the bombs that he could warn the men there was one on the way before they knew themselves. He could also sense the presence of any insurgents before they had chance to attack. Having him around on night patrols became invaluable as his detection skills were heightened after dark and soldiers from many regiments said they felt safer with Tangye in their party. Rik Groves had always felt that way about his dog on night patrols but there he was still helping people years later.

Mascots are held in high regard by the humans who serve with them. But a mascot who stands beside them in the line of fire is regarded as exceptional. Even in the early days, the well-mannered, if not always well-behaved, Tangye had the gift to bridge any gap in a relationship. He bonded with the men of OMLT and the series of regiments they were attached to. He provided an unusual bridge between the Nato Forces and the local people of Kajaki. The dog's habit of getting everywhere soon made even the most stubborn dog hater's heart melt. The village elders who encountered Tangye were slowly but surely exposed to the dog's friendly antics and some opened their doors to the animal the Taliban labelled 'dirty'. Such significant cultural moves were important and Tangye's personality made them possible. The fact that he had been taught to shake a paw with a human was impressive and, although the locals may have thought it silly and strange to begin, with they were astonished that such training was possible. Tangye was a star in a way that only a dog could be.

But there were big concerns for Tangye's safety. He was now known to be bold in the face of battle and had gained a reputation for being fearless under fire but the increased use of IEDs and the success of the enemy's ambushes put Tangye's life in danger. There was a serious growing concern for the dog's safety.

When Military Policeman Corporal Sam Hendley arrived in Kajaki on 16 October 2009, it was to take over the role of lone policeman attached to the regiment C Company, 3rd Battalion The Rifles. Like many soldiers entering Kajaki, he had heard of Tangye and was looking out for him. He didn't have to wait longer than his first day. As he collected his pistol and extra socks from stores, he saw Tangye running with his little dog gang. He would soon realize that Tangye and Gaydog were inseparable. For the next two months (October and November 2009), Sam had the pleasure of patrolling with Tangye and he said it was as if the dog had picked him out of the ranks and spoke to him softly, 'Tangye must have sensed my anxiety because he looked at me like an old soldier as if to say, "Don't worry, I know you're new to this but I've done it a million times and you will be all right." I know he was a dog but I needed some reassurance and Tangye was there for me.'

If there was one place Tangye loved being more than any other it was on patrol with the soldiers. And the feeling was mutual. But 3 Rifles were about to complete their tour of duty and there was a feeling in the ranks that Tangye's bold behaviour in the line of fire would one day prove his undoing. He had gained a reputation for being fearless under fire and this attitude was the greatest morale boost when the troops needed it most but it was also dangerous. No one wanted him to be shot after the support he had provided as a mascot and all the goodwill he had fostered by being a dog like no other. There was talk of sending him 'home'. Not to a shelter in Afghanistan but to a home in Britain.

When Sam Hendley heard that there were plans to move Tangye for his own safety he, like many soldiers in Kajaki, was apprehensive for the dog. And, at the back of his mind, there was also a selfish thought: what would life on camp be like without Tangye? He was still just a big puppy and full of mischief. His sweet vulnerability was part of his appeal but it was his cheekiness that made him a real hit with almost everyone. Even at four years old he would still ambush anyone for a taste of their ration packs. If there was food around, he would wait to be offered a share but if nothing was forthcoming he would beg or steal it anyway.

Tangye was not just the resident comedian he was the comforter too. Sam Hendley remembers, 'On 20 December 2009, when I was called into the Operations Room I knew it had to be bad news. It was the worst. A fellow military policeman had been killed. I was about to go on duty and could not help wondering if today could be my turn to go out and not come back. The emotion of the news got the better of me and I'm still not sure how or where he came from, but suddenly Tangye was with me. He came to me, settled his head on my lap and stayed.'

The dangers were increasing for Tangye as they were for the men. The dreaded IEDs were now a constant daily threat to safety and Tangye's habit of running ahead of everyone was going to put him in direct danger. The men of 3 Rifles did not want to leave him behind but the military could not confirm that the dog would be protected after they left. He was an Afghan-born dog and there was a fear that he would either be stoned to death or turned loose to return to his old life of fending for himself on the sands of Kajaki. He was so used to human company that he would assume all humans were kind and discover they are not. If he was going to be rescued from an uncertain future how could it be done?

As far as the soldiers were concerned, it seemed there was only one thing to do – attract public support. When the national newspapers reported Tangye's plight and the need to get him out of Kajaki for safety's sake, the ball started to roll. Natalie Pomroy of Labrador Links Rescue saw the pictures of Tangye in the newspaper and immediately started a Facebook campaign. She contacted Pen Farthing, founder of NOWZAD, the charity that had already successful sprung several Afghanistan-based dogs and cats to the safety of British shores. In the press, a Lance Corporal Brent Meheux said they wanted the dog out and safe because he had meant so much to them when they had been in Afghanistan, 'When the lads were under fire he would run up and down the line barking and wagging his tail. It was as if he was shouting encouragement.'

Pen Farthing, himself a former Royal Marine Commando, understood exactly how the soldiers felt; it was why he formed NOWZAD to help such cases. But his intelligence network in Kajaki said the dog was too far into insurgent country to get out successfully. They knew he was there but he could not be reached without risking the exposure of the people who moved the dogs around. And even if they could get the dog into a position to lift out, there was still the matter of finances to cover the cost of the local drivers and the paperwork and flights to enter the UK. This operation had to be executed with stealth and military precision planning for the protection of everyone involved, including Tangye.

The media had taken Tangye to its heart and so had the supporters of the Labrador Link Facebook page. Within an hour of launching her page, Natalie had 500 members all wanting to support the campaign to bring Tangye to the safety of the UK. By January 2010, the campaign was gathering momentum and had raised over £5,000 towards the moving and administrative costs. A letter from Prime Minister Gordon Brown declining to assist Tangye's passage to the UK only fired the determination of everyone involved to get the dog out as soon as was humanly possible. Each of the dogs rescued from Afghanistan is the subject of a covert operation that takes place over several days and sometimes weeks and Pen Farthing co-ordinates the rescue with the minimum of people. The difference with Tangye was that by the time he could be safely reached, thousands of people were waiting for news of his rescue. For the safety of everyone involved this rescue had to be one of Pen's most secret.

It was in March 2010 that Tangye 'disappeared' from the Kajaki camp. It was possible due to the remote location from which the military lifted Tangye by helicopter to Kandahar but after that the full-on rescue was down to local help. The next part of his journey was by road and on one of the most dangerous stretches in Helmand from Kandahar to the Afghan rescue centre, which was in a secret location. The Taliban's dedication to targeting aid workers as mich as soldiers has demanded the need for much secrecy. British rescue worker Louise Hastie met Tangye off the helicopter and kept him for two days before he started his long journey by road. The local drivers risked their livelihood and often their lives on these trips. Littered with Afghan checkpoints the road would be a constant challenge to the driver; he knew that if he was stopped and the dog was discovered he would be severely beaten for helping a Western operation. The dog was likely to be shot too.

Tangye was very quiet as he took his place in the back of the truck. Louise had checked him over to confirm that he was fit enough for the trip. It was not usual to see him so quiet but everything was strange for a dog who was used to the desert as his back garden. There would be no drink stops or comfort breaks along the way for Tangye. Pen and the local team were worried that if the driver was seen walking the dog or even stopping to offer him water the consequences would be dire. The risk of Tangye wandering off was also too great. It was a foregone conclusion that he would not come back to the driver. The relief of arriving at the rescue centre must have been huge for both dog and driver. After food and drink, Tangye enjoyed his first game of football for several days. He was now just days away from his flight 'home'.

Boarding the commercial flight bound for Heathrow, Tangye was quiet and well behaved. It's possible that his soldier friends in 3 Rifles wouldn't recognize this quiet dog as their Tangye but then their dog had never been on a helicopter, on a long road trip, in a kennel or long haul on an aircraft. This was all new to this brave Labrador.

After the formalities at Heathrow, Tangye headed for the quarantine kennels. In the meantime, his new friend Jean Henman at Labrador Retriever Rescue Southern England was working on his new home. There was one thing for sure, it had to have lots of space even if it lacked the sand of Kajaki.

Tangye arrived in the UK on the 24 March 2010. He was now a free and safe dog. As Pen Farthing of NOWZAD says: 'Dogs and cats don't have a voice in all of this but it's more than likely that this dog would have died if he had been abandoned to life in the Afghan desert. These animals cannot stand up for themselves and they are helpless in war. It's the people in power making the decisions and others are left to help the victims. Tangye has made the biggest journey in his life and he is now safe.'

For Rik Groves, the man who handed over the ten dollars for the scrap of a Labrador puppy, to have the dog in safety in Britain was a huge relief. 'As speculation over Tangye's safety grew, it was right the men wanted to guarantee his passage home. There were so many dogs out there who didn't make it, for one reason or another, and we could not let that happen to Tangye. If we had, we would never have forgiven ourselves.'

One of the rules of conflict is to maintain morale and dogs adopted by the soldiers serving in Afghanistan certainly raise spirits. When the men discovered that Tangye had been lifted out, there was a feeling of emptiness and then relief that he would now be safe. There's a military motto that in conflict no one is left behind and Pen Farthing and NOWZAD are working on making that true for dogs befriended by service personnel too. We know that of course not every one can make that journey but those who can will and that is reassurance for sure, especially when we know that as long as there are British soldiers serving in Afghanistan there will be dogs there too.

Sergeant Stubby –

The Most
Decorated Dog
in History

'A dog?' replied Private Conroy.
'This is no dog. This is a war hero.'

(Private J. Robert Conroy – 102nd Infantry, 26th 'Yankee' Division,

First World War veteran and master of Stubby, canine hero of the trenches.

Smithsonian records.)

The elegant lobby of the Hotel Majestic in New York teamed with activity. Honoured to be hosting a reception for homegrown heroes of the First World War, staff had rolled out the red carpet to welcome their distinguished guests. But what was that scruffy looking dog doing there? The staff scurried around and quickly drew lots to decide which one of them was going to tell the veteran soldier, his chest was bristling with medals, that his Bull Terrier was not welcome in the hotel.

The job fell to the manager who glanced down at the elderly looking dog in the unusual leather coat as he announced, 'I'm sorry, sir, but dogs are not allowed in this hotel.'

It was a pity the manager had not taken a closer look at the dog's coat. If he had spared a moment he would have seen that it was covered in military honours. If he had bothered to ask, he would have been told that the dog had survived seventeen of the bloodiest battles in the last eighteen months of the war and saved countless lives by detecting the first whiff of the invisible toxic gasses that plagued the trenches and the far-away howl of an approaching shell. Gassed, shelled, shot at and traumatized, Stubby survived it all. A soldier dog suffering as the men were suffering.

Private John Robert Conroy reeled back and gathered his breath, 'A dog?' he replied …

The story of Stubby is legendary. He was a not very big stray dog from nowhere, adopted by a young American soldier. They both ended up in the trenches of the Western Front in 1917 and both survived against all the odds. Their story is a testament to devotion and companionship, faith and love.

It all began on the campus of Yale University where the 1st Connecticut Regiment from Hartford area and the 2nd Connecticut Regiment from New Haven had been sent for training ahead of being deployed to France to assist in the war against Germany. The two forces were short of the 1,000 men required to form a regiment and so they were combined to become the 102nd Infantry and part of the 26th 'Yankee' Division of Massachusetts. One of the young recruits was John Robert Conroy. Conroy had decided, along with an increasing number of men of his age, that joining the ranks of the United States Army, Navy or its embryonic aviation unit was a duty to their country. By April 1917, when America entered the

Great War, as it was known then, these men were to form the backbone of the first deployment of US infantry.

America was at war despite the efforts of its President, Woodrow Wilson, to keep them out of what appeared to be a European conflict. But it was the British Royal Navy's secret code breaking unit – Cryptanalytic, Room 40 – that broke the German diplomatic code and intercepted a message that the US Government simply could not ignore and that was destined to change the course of the war. The message was a proposal from Berlin to Mexico suggesting that if the US decided to join the war then Mexico should join too but not as her ally but as the Keiser's ally and that together they should then enlist Japan. Such an alliance would make it impossible for the US to take its eye off its own shores or deploy troops to Europe. The effective slowing of the Allies' offensive would then give Germany the breathing space it needed to launch a fleet of submarines that could strangle Britain by cutting off valuable supplies. And the payback? If Mexico offered its support then Germany would help reclaim territory lost seventy years before in the Mexican-American War, land that included Texas, North Mexico and Arizona. The deal was there in black and white and once revealed, the Zimmermann Telegram, as it became known, could not be ignored. Wilson may have won his presidency on the strength of his anti-war stance but now he was forced to use this damaging document to build support for and to justify America joining Britain and France against Germany. The President could no longer hold fast to neutrality as a defence. He called for war and on 6 April 1917, the US Congress declared the country's entry into the Great War.

Although America had not officially participated in the war from its declaration in 1914, many US citizens had joined the war effort in the only ways open to them: they could join a British regiment if they had the appropriate family connections or they could sign up with the French Foreign Legion and use that route to fight with the Allied Forces. The drive to join up increased throughout 1916 and James Robert Conroy was as enthusiastic as the next man to be part of a great victory in Europe and he joined the 26th 'Yankee' Division as they set up their encampment and started their training in the vicinity of the Yale Bowl.

When basic training permitted, the recruits were allowed into town in the evening to unwind and have some fun and it was then the young Private Conroy noticed a yellowish dog begging for attention and food. The dog did not have the look of a scared and downtrodden street dog. He was different. Certainly not handsome but obviously full of spirit and character, the dog was mostly American Bull Terrier with maybe a strain of Bulldog thrown in. He had the breed's determined, jutting jaw and proportionately small, pointed ears. His stout, solid body was covered in short bristled hair which was the shade of wet sand.

Yes, he was a little shabby but he was proud and carried himself well. He had the bearing of an aristocrat who had temporarily fallen on hard times.

'Hey, Conroy. Do you see that dog over there?' a fellow recruit said. 'Have you noticed it's been following you?' The young army volunteer had noticed the dog out of the corner of his eye and it seemed that as soon as the soldier appeared the dog did too. In the town, on the sports field or during training at some point, he would be there. Conroy found himself looking out for the dog and sooner or later he always turned up. The dog knew where to find the man and one afternoon he decided he would come and wait for him at the main gates to the camp. Everyone who saw him sitting there so patiently guessed he was waiting for Conroy and sure enough, when the soldier appeared, the dog gave him a crazy welcome. It was the first defining moment in their relationship.

For Conroy, just the sight of the dog sitting waiting for him was enough to prompt a big decision. He was going to adopt the sandy dog, there and then and take him into the camp. It was a bold thing to do as he knew pets were not allowed on site and he had no idea how much longer they would be there before being shipped overseas. He didn't know if he would be allowed to keep his new friend but he was going to try. He smuggled the dog into the barracks where he made a bed for him under his own bunk. Finding a name for a dog with a stubby tail was easy. Stubby had arrived and Stubby was there to stay. All Conroy had to do was keep him safe and, for the moment, that meant keeping him hidden.

It was lucky for Conroy that his sergeant was a dog lover and intelligent enough to see that Stubby was a huge morale boost to the men. He was furious when he discovered that the dog's name had been added to the regimental strength but soon realized that it was not worth admonishing the men for doing all they could to protect their unofficial mascot. Instead, the sergeant decided to turn a blind eye to Stubby's presence and so it was that the mascot dog joined the men in everything they did, including full combat training.

Stubby was exposed to the deafening clout of ammunition and exploding shells. He learnt to drop down and crawl along, his stomach brushing on the ground, as the men did the same beside him. The more he heard the high-pitched whining of the shells, the quicker his reactions became. He was never scared and never ran from Conroy's side, no matter how loud the battle noise. He very quickly developed a sense for detecting the shells overhead long before the men could hear them. Picking up the distant whine, Stubby would drop down and freeze in this position. Months later, in the trenches of France, this would become a very useful early warning

system for his infantry friend and many men had Stubby
to thank for saving their lives. But at that moment on the
training ground at Yale, the dog's habit of putting his
paws over his ears just before an explosion seemed like
nothing more than an amusing party trick.

Stubby had been Conroy's partner for almost a year
when the presidential decree for general mobilization of
troops was signed in May 1917. By then Stubby was used
to all the bugle calls, drills, marches and routines of camp
life. He could even salute. Mimicking the men, he put his
right paw up to his eyebrow and each time he did it he
impressed his audience. After a year in the company of
the 26th 'Yankee' Division, Stubby was as much a soldier
as any of the men and they recognized him in that way
too. There was no way Conroy, or any of the others, was
going to leave Stubby behind when they shipped out to
Europe so a plan was devised to smuggle the dog onto
the truck leaving the camp and then the train to the transport ship, the *SS Minnesota,* bound for France.

There was no problem getting Stubby past their own
sergeant but the transport ship guards would have plenty
to say if they discovered a Bull Terrier hidden in someone's kit bag. And that was another problem: Stubby was
too big to hide in a bag. The best chance the men had of
disguising the dog was to make him look like an extra, if
very small, human. Under the cover of Conroy's greatcoat, the dog was successfully transferred on board and

then into the ship's coal bin where he spent the first twelve hours of the journey. One of the men watched the door at all times, until Conroy felt they were far enough out to sea to let him out. But he was still careful to keep Stubby under wraps – it was unbearable to even imagine that, given an unsympathetic commanding officer, the men could be ordered to throw their dog overboard. But they were lucky. The officers who did catch a glimpse of Stubby when he took his strolls on deck did nothing to harm him. They could see how valuable the little animal was to the men and right there and then in the confines of the ship he was safe. And although it must have been a very uncomfortable journey for everyone, the men were entertained by Stubby who had acquired a set of soldier's dog tags made for him by one of the ship's machinists. It was a gift that told the dog, 'You're a soldier now.'

Conroy's army-issue greatcoat was to come in handy again at the other end of this long journey – to smuggle Stubby off the *SS Minnesota*. Wrapped like a small person in the long wool coat, Stubby knew instinctively to stay quiet as they were, by no means, home and dry. It was a miracle that Stubby had survived the journey from the US to France, not just because it was fraught with the danger of him being discovered but because of the unhealthy way the men were packed on board the ship.

By the time they reached their final destination, soldiers and dog alike were more than ready to disembark. But, for the men of the 102nd Infantry, their patience needed to last out a little longer until they were on their way to the camp. It was there that Conroy met their commanding officer who took one look at Stubby and asked how on earth the private had gotten this far with a dog all the way from Yale Field, Connecticut. Conroy had nothing to lose now, except the most precious companion he had known so he explained how Stubby had befriended him and become such a very special member of the division. Stubby was happy to salute on command and the CO could see that the dog was well behaved and loyal. As Conroy held his breath, almost expecting the officer to issue an order to abandon the dog, the decision came to make Stubby the mascot of the 102nd Infantry, 26th 'Yankee' Division and with that status he would be able to accompany the men into the trenches and see active service at their side. Conroy could not have wished for a better outcome. His relief was almost tangible.

It was October 1917, and the American Expeditionary Forces were beginning to enter the battlefields of the Western Front. They had no idea what they were about to face or the unimaginable horror they were to experience.

The war had been raging for three years and most of the idyllic French countryside had been utterly devastated.

The war-torn landscape resembled a moonscape. Craters made by shells designed to rip up the earth and anyone in their path covered the ground for as far as the eye could see. The devastation caused in battle was reflected on the land; huge areas blackened by the unrelenting bombardment of shells, machine guns and flame throwers were bare of living things. There was no green on the ground or on the stricken trees, only grey ash and the charred remains of the living.

The young soldiers from America arrived with drive and enthusiasm to see justice done and the perpetrators put in their place. But what they found on the ground was a battle plan that had made no sense for three years and resulted in the deaths of millions of people. The 26th 'Yankee' Division had their first glimpse of the Western Front on a chill October morning. They were one of the first US Forces to land in France and the first thing that hit them was the cold. Led by Douglas MacArthur (who was to make a name for himself later as one of the foremost generals of the Second World War and the War in the Pacific), the men marched up the line as best they could in the muddy conditions and stood to attention to wait for further orders.

That first view of the Western Front was a sight that would remain with the survivors for the rest of their lives. The ground that had been churned over by shells, tanks and the charge of cavalry horses had now absorbed the autumn rains covering everything as far as the eye could see into an ocean of thick, yellow mud. The soldiers trudged through the mire towards their designated spot passing the line of field hospitals as they went. Seeing the vast number of casualties and their horrific injuries was not good for the morale of men who had been on the front for less than twenty-four hours. The dead and the dying lay everywhere. The pitiful sight of horses drown in the mud, their nostrils flared as they took their last breath from the surface.

It was this kind of horror that had Conroy holding on extra tight to Stubby, the dog he was carrying safely in his arms. Wading through the mire, Conroy made a silent promise to his friend: 'I will not let anything happen to you. I promise I will get you home safe and to live a life beyond this hell of war.' Stubby looked at Conroy as if he understood every word. It was a knowing look that the soldier would see on his dog's face many times and one he came to rely on in moments when despair could have taken hold. He reached that emotional black spot many times but Stubby was always there to bring him back from the brink.

A great deal of coffee was consumed and cigarettes smoked as the men stood around the camp braziers waiting for their orders. The winter of 1917–18 was particularly harsh and it was enough for the men to do to wait and keep warm and alive. The mud fields of the

Champagne Marne, where they were dug in at the front line, were now frozen solid and this made the task of moving heavy artillery virtually impossible. During the autumn rains, the heavy gun carriages had lodged fast in the mud and many sank taking the horses and the men – who were trying to the last to get the horses free – with them.

When the churned-over earth froze, the hard peaks and deep troughs claimed the transport in a different way, running it aground. Any thaw caused the water to trickle down the sides of the trenches and create a wall and a floor of thick ice overnight. The trenches were just six to eight feet wide and retained whatever fell both day and night: snow, rain, ice – it all lingered there to torment the soldiers. The incredible cold took away any feeling they had in their fingers and toes while the constant thud of artillery deadened any ability to process thoughts.

Here there was no escaping the harshness of the winter and how Conroy saved Stubby from dying from exposure is anyone's guess. But whatever shelter he created and however many blankets he borrowed, he kept Stubby alive. On 5 February 1918, the 102nd Infantry moved to the front line at the Chemin des Dames, Stubby alongside them. He could have felt in no doubt that he was amongst friends and Conroy was his master.

This was Stubby's first taste of conflict and he adapted to its noises and smells without a whimper. The almost constant snap of the rifles and roar of the heavy artillery fire did not appear to phase him. Maybe the exposure he had in training was enough to give him confidence. But this time the ammunition was real not dummy. The snipers were German crack shots and the exchange of fire between the trenches was capable of taking life – and frequently did.

In March 1918, a change in the weather gave the Germans exactly what they wanted. Months of freezing snow and thick ice meant any chance of a German offensive had been frustrated. Now, with the great melt underway, the German Army focussed its sights on a massive offensive against the British, Canadian, French and American Forces facing them. The spring offensive got underway with everything being thrown at the Allies in an attempt to break them down. At this time, a quarter of a million US soldiers were being sent to fight the war overseas every month. And although many were inexperienced, they made up for it with gallons of sheer enthusiasm. The emphasis was to get as many men as possible overseas so any form of training was short and basic. A rifle and a bayonet were the soldiers' essentials. And the idea was to get into the war and get it finished as it had already gone on far longer than the Allies expected. But they were about to meet a new enemy – trench gas.

Mustard gas had been in use early on in the war and, discovering how effective it was, the chemical properties were enhanced to add phosgene, chlorine and a mix called yperite to the list of toxic clouds that were released into the trenches. Gas was effective because it was a silent killer. It always achieved the element of surprise. Hardly discernable from the early morning mist, the gas rolled into the trenches, its odour blending with an atmosphere soaked in the stench of cordite. Creeping in, it insidiously attacked the soldiers' eyes, burnt their skin and had them tearing at their chests to catch a breath of air. Blistered skin, blindness, and the respiratory effects of shrivelled lungs were just some of the problems inflicted by the trench gasses. Crude gas masks were hastily invented with versions for the dogs and horses in the trenches too. But often it was too little too late; the damage had already been done and casualties lay strewn in the trenches, writhing and shouting in pain as the toxic cloud descended on them. The men clung to each other, unable to see a hand before their face. Rescued by the field medics, the men would be led away in lines holding on to each other for support.

Stubby's sensitive nose was onto the first whiff of chemicals that came anywhere near his trench. At first, Conroy and rest of the men did not know what the dog was trying to tell as he ran up and down the trench barking but, after one experience of not following his warning, they never made the mistake again. One morning, as the early mist clung to the top of the trenches, Stubby awoke with a start. Conroy was by his side, sleeping the sleep of a man weary from the fight. Sniper fire had been heavy during the previous evening and that had followed a bombardment of artillery throughout the day. Sometimes sleep was the only escape. But not this time. Stubby sensed something; he pushed his head up to the sky and leant back. Sniffing the air he began to yelp. When yelping didn't raise anyone, he began to bark loudly, leaping around Conroy as he slept. Louder and louder Stubby barked. He ran along the trench making enough noise to attract everyone's attention. He had to wake Conroy before it was too late to put on a gasmask.

'Hey Stubby, what's your problem?' Conroy asked, concered. By this time the dog had buried his head under his blanket but he was still barking the warning. By the time the soldier realized what was going on, Stubby's whole body was under the blanket. Only his stubby tail was visible. 'My God, it's a gas attack,' shouted Conroy. 'Stubby, stay …!'

Conroy alerted the men and the gasmasks were deployed. But it was too late for some; the gas had got into their lungs and their eyes. It was a horrid sight to witness. But Stubby had tried to warn them and Conroy was aware of that. His 'call' was way ahead of the human warning call of 'Gas! Gas!' That call came far too late for many. That day Stubby saved his master and many of the 26th 'Yankee' Division and he would save many more over the months to come. No one ever ignored the dog again.

The Americans were eager to fight. The 102nd Infantry had waited three months to put their training into action and in the Battle of Schieprey they had their chance. Here the US met the might of the German Guards renowned for their indomitable strength, and held out to retain the town. It was an enormous challenge for the comparatively inexperienced American Expeditionary Force but there was only one way to overcome them and that was to meet them head on. With Stubby ordered to stay in the trench, the men prepared to stand their ground. They had turned the direction of the battle and now the Germans were withdrawing. Stubby sensed the excitement of the battle and, as if he knew his friends were reaching victory, he leapt onto the top of the trenches jumping about and barking as the Germans and Allies exchanged grenades. Surrounded by explosions, Stubby barked encouragement to the men who were positioned at Dead Man's Curve on the road outside Schieprey.

'Stubby, get down from there,' Conroy shouted when he saw Stubby bounding over the top of the trench. 'Get down!' Maybe Stubby hadn't heard his master over the repeated grenade explosions and when he did, it was too late. A grenade left the hands of a German soldier, aimed at Stubby. The dog didn't see it coming. As it fell at Stubby's feet, it exploded. Fortunately, he was darting away towards Conroy and the blast only glanced his front legs. Conroy saw his dog fall and ran in to grab him. Taking him in his arms, he laid him down on the dog's makeshift bed and then carried on with the fight. Once over and the enemy put on the run, Conroy collected Stubby in his arms and sought out the medic.

The field hospitals were always brimming and there was no end to the stream of casualties. All of the injuries inflicted were a reflection of the ferocity of the ammunition and equipment being used. The First World War was fought with twentieth-century technology but nineteenth-century tactics; the result was the death of millions. By the end of 1917, the battles were still fought between trenches with a no-man's-land bridging the space between them but the necessities of war had resulted in a number of crucial developments: field telephone systems, wireless communication, armoured cars, tanks and then aircraft. At the outbreak of war in 1914, the heavy artillery on the front line consisted of canons. By 1917, this had developed into a combination of automatic rifles, mortars, machine guns and 'big' guns such as Big Bertha and the Germans' Paris Gun. On the ground, the tank and the flame thrower cut ghastly scars into the earth. The tank could not outrun the horse but it could crush anything in its path. The flame thrower could either wipe out its operator (if not handled carefully) or the occupants of an entire trench in the most efficient and horrific way. At sea, submarines lay in wait for the opportunity to dominate the waves. In the air, Zeppelins and the first fighter planes made a tentative step into the theatre of war. And back on the ground, infantry formations were reorganized too. Companies of a hundred men were unwieldy: squads of ten or so men under the command of a junior NCO were preferred. Lessons were being learnt and approaches refined but this only increased the death toll. In the four months of the Battle of the Somme (July to November 1916), history recorded 1.5 million casualties. It was only one of the bloodiest of the Great War.

There was never a respite from the treatment of the injured and sick so the addition of one dog with shrapnel wounds was no problem. If there was a group of people who understood the value of the mascot dog in the throes of war, it was the medics. Stubby's injuries landed him a transfer to the Red Cross field hospital for several days. During that time he became their most popular patient. He not only recovered from his own shrapnel wounds but he helped others overcome their pain, fear and anxiety too. He was a great morale boost to the men in the trenches and his presence in the hospital was possibly more valuable to some than medication. Having Stubby's happy, smiling face and ever-friendly personality on hand in such grim surroundings must have proven to many that a dog really can be man's best friend.

Returning to the trenches, Stubby was welcomed by his master Private James Robert Conroy and the rest of the 26th 'Yankee' Division. The men had not realized how much they could miss their mascot until he was away from them for just a few days. The dog had a wonderful welcome from all his friends and it was just what he needed to settle him back into trench routine and the daily dice with death by bullet, gas, mortar or the new enemy – Spanish influenza. The disease swept through the trenches on both sides and took civilian victims too. The epidemic killed 60,000 Americans alone.

The military onslaught was relentless. It was now May 1918 and there was no sign of a let-up. The German Army was closing in on Paris and considering an early celebration of victory. They did not see the new influx from the US as a threat to their march into the capital. Unfortunately for the Kaiser's men, the idea of Paris falling to the enemy only strengthened their resolve and they rallied as the Second Battle of the Marne got underway.

The battle became a showcase for all the artillery and chemical weapons the Allies and the Germans had to offer. As each side threw all they had at the opposing side, the trenches were crawling with activity. The snipers' bullets flew and mustard gas was released to deplete the infantry. For a while, the two forces were matched for strength and locked in combat. Day and night the guns pounded incessantly. The orange flashes as the shells hit their target filled the sky until there was nothing but clouds of drifting, grey smoke as far as the eye could see. Through the haze the machine guns rattled and the screams of men falling in agony punctured the air. Stubby was not afraid of the guns but the crazy, confusion of battle caused him to howl in what sounded like anger. As he dashed from one part of the line to another, it was as if his performance was to rouse the troops like a bark of encouragement. He could not take up arms to assist them but what the men wanted was their mascot's loyalty, cheerfulness and comfort. And they received that in spades.

If Stubby was ever absent from Conroy's side it would be because he was with a wounded soldier in the field, a corner of the trench or dugout. He had an ability to seek out the injured on a battlefield and instinctively knew that he had to comfort them. Many a dying soldier's last words were uttered to this loyal dog; words that may never have been spoken or shared with a human companion. He licked their faces and rested his paws on their hands as if to offer a close comfort. And the men reached out for the dog's warmth and attention. They told him of their loved ones and the things they missed from home. They told him all that flashed before them in their final moments. Dogs will never repeat a secret or admonish a harsh word. For Conroy to share his dog in this was very special and everyone appreciated his generosity of spirit. Conroy had to become accustomed to the fact that, if his dog was missing, he could be sitting in no-man's-land with another soldier awaiting the arrival of the stretcher bearers. Stubby soon learnt to recognize the ambulance crews and the first aiders and would let out a low bark to alert them to a casualty.

Ironically, the more Stubby became the shared companion of the 26th 'Yankee' Division and the heavier the battle became, the stronger the bond between Conroy and his faithful dog grew. Under the strain of battle, there was something that made them feel mutually responsible for each other. What had started as an accidental friendship was now a partnership strengthened by hardship and the pressure to protect was running high. 'Stubby, stay close now. Don't wander,' Conroy was often heard saying. The soldier was afraid the dog would be too far away for him to protect if there was a gas attack and he needed his mask. And he was right to worry. No sooner had the words left his mouth than Conroy felt Stubby shuffling out of his grasp. Stubby could sense something his master could not.

Wrestling free of Conroy's grasp, Stubby stood square and pushed his head up and back as far as it would go. He sniffed the air. Suddenly he started to bark and run round until he had Conroy's full attention. Then he started his routine of burying his body under clothing or in stores or whatever was lying about until only his hind-quarters were visible. By now, the men knew exactly what was going on. 'Gas! Gas! Gas!' the call went down the line as gasmasks were pulled on before the whiff of mustard gas had a chance to cause any harm to the men. Several minutes later, the morning mist took on a ghostly pallor and picked up pace moving into the dips and gulleys of the trenches. 'Gas! Gas!' a runner called, appearing out of the ghostly gloom with the warning that would have been too late for many.

Stubby's gift for giving advance warning of a gas attack was partly due to personal experience – he had been gassed himself. It was only on one occasion but the experience left its mark. As the unit was advancing over open ground, a gas shell landed and broke by Stubby's paws. He had no chance of escaping the poisonous cloud. Conroy picked up his beloved dog in his arms and ran back to the trenches where the medic was called. Stubby's eyes were deeply affected: the gas had sealed his eyelids shut and they were oozing horribly. There was nothing Conroy or his team of dedicated helpers could do but continue to bathe his eyes and wait for signs of recovery. Stubby lay on his cot for days without moving. He did not respond to the gentle touch of the soldiers tending to him. He could not even manage a whimper. The sadness was overwhelming for Private Conroy. He feared the worst and wished that he could conjure up a picture of his dog running free and happy on the Yale Field. All he needed was a sign to give him a glimmer of hope and, after a week of stillness and silence, he got it. One evening, as the soldier sat by his dog talking to him about happier times and familiar things, an incredible thing happened: Stubby wagged the stump of his tail. It must have taken enormous effort on the dog's part, he was so weak. Conroy could not help but shed a tear of relief.

During the time he had been ill, Stubby had, once again, visited his friends in the casualty centre where surgical operations were taking place all day and night in addition to the many cases requiring bandaging and bathing. Once again, Stubby was made welcome and as soon as he was feeling better he started to wander amongst the patients, cheering them up and being the centre of attention. They loved him! No matter how ill the patients were, they would try to reach out to stroke the dog. He was the best distraction from pain and the best form of medication known to man. Some in the hospital had this dog to thank for either finding them on the battlefield and bringing help or barking an air-raid warning or gas alert. This dog was a friend and a lifesaver. He was becoming famous among the troops along the front line.

Every effort from the Germans to shut down the Allied Force crumbled with the Second Battle of the Marne. Despite their high hopes to use the Spring Offensive to crush the British and American troops, the Germans failed. Even their highly trained Storm Troopers were put under pressure by the relatively inexperienced US troops and sent into retreat. Still, there seemed no let-up in the march for glory. Millions already been killed and yet no lessons had been learnt from the disaster at Gallipoli, the many months of hell played out at Ypres, the yellow mud of the Somme and the seemingly never-ending campaign in Verdun. With neither side showing signs of superiority or ultimate strength it was likely the US joining the war could be mistaken for more cannon fodder for the German machine guns. Nothing had been solved and the two sides remained locked along rigid lines that ran from the Belgian-French border on the Channel to Luxembourg and the German border.

Peace remained elusive but the thirst for victory intensified on both sides. By the time the fighting commenced in Chateau Thierry in June 1918, the intense focus on the use of artillery was taking its toll on the troops and the environment. Shells blew deep holes in the earth and buried or split open the soldiers who ventured into their path. The sight of trees blown completely out of the ground or covered in soldiers' remains was something the survivors would replay in their nightmares for years to come. This pretty French town was scarred by the war and to help win it back for the Allies the Americans drafted in more of their countrymen. African-American regiments were called up to do their duty serving with the French troops. It gave units like the Harlem Hellfighters (the 93rd Infantry Division) a chance to live up to their name – they were certainly being posted to the nearest place anyone could imagine to a hell on earth. Serving with the French 16th Division, this unit went on to receive the Croix de Guerre for its action in Chateau Thierry.

The Americans were to engage in a series of pitched battles and Stubby would play his part, showing every time an amazing allegiance to his master. One day, as the units advanced over open, shell-cratered ground, the artillery bombardment was heavy and unrelenting. Suddenly, the men saw Stubby hit the ground and for one terrible second Conroy thought he had been hit. But then the dog's front paws went up over his ears and his stubby tail stuck out behind him. Seconds later, a huge explosion hit with earsplitting effect. Conroy was on the floor, thrown and stunned but impressed with his dog's actions. Stubby had sensed the oncoming shell and if the men had been watching him they could have all hit the ground well ahead of the explosions. From that moment on, the troops stayed close to Stubby because as their advanced warning system he would inevitably save lives. Conroy could not have been more pleased with and proud of his dog.

The Second Battle of Marne had instigated an offensive by the Allied Forces which would became their first major and victorious offensive of the war. The Hundred Day Offensive started on 8 August 1918 and it would prove to be a black day for the German Army who were now beginning to realize the counterattacks by the Allies were becoming more decisive. By 18 September and the start of the Battle of St Mihiel, south-west of Verdun, the combined forces of the Americans, French and Canadians were ready to help turn the tide of the war. For the first time, the infantry were supported by an air strike of 1,000 aircraft and together they destroyed the German presence. It was the final time in the Great War that territory was deliberately recaptured from the Germans.

By 11 November 1918, the Germans had surrendered and the Armistice was signed in a railway carriage specially sited in the woods of Compiegne, near Beauvais. There was no further need to slice away territory and fight to take it back. It was all over. Or so it seemed.

While the bulk of the Allied Forces were going through the motions of the Armistice, American Forces were still entrenched at the confluence of Meuse and Argonne. It was the last stand of the war and in the

desperate throes of the action to retain and regain territory and dignity, the frantic gunfire and grenade attacks
were still taking lives. It was ironic that all through their
eighteen months together in a foreign country and
engaged in hostile activities, it was only in the last days of
these horrific hostilities that Private Conroy sustained a
serious head injury. A stray bullet embedded itself in
Conroy's skull and almost before he hit the ground
Stubby was at his master's side. He was used to tending
to casualties by sitting with them and licking their
wounds but this time the dog was agitated and only paci-
fied when the stretcher bearers arrived to take Conroy to
the field hospital.

Throughout his primary treatment, Stubby was alongside his master and no more than a whisker's width away
from him at all times. The aftercare was very protracted
but that was not a problem as long as man and dog
remained together. Lying with Conroy gave Stubby an
opportunity to comfort other soldiers being brought in
for treatment. Stubby would see them arrive on stretch-
ers and then move in alongside them so he could lick
their face, arms, hands, his big, rough tongue giving sign
of affection and care. Stubby's lick was often a reviving
sensation and the one fond thing patients remembered
when they woke.

Of course, Conroy received five-star treatment from
Stubby during the time they were stretchered off the field

and the weeks they were in the medical centre. But when it was decided the private should be moved to the American Hospital in Paris there was a doubt whether Stubby would be allowed to go too. It was one thing for field hospitals to accept mascot dogs but quite a different one for those hospitals located away from the front. Fortunately, the doctor in charge of Conroy's case recognized the value of keeping this man and this dog together and pleaded the case with everyone he needed to. And Stubby, while licking his master's hand, knew exactly what he had to do to cajole the medics into allowing him to travel with his master: just be his normal adoring self. And it worked. The soldier and his faithful Bull Terrier were bound for Paris in an ambulance that rocked and shook but still managed to get dog and patient where they needed to be and in a bed for the night.

Stubby had acquired a kind of celebrity status since the moment he joined the Army and went to war. The way Conroy and his fellow soldiers treated the dog with care and respect made onlookers aware that this dog was highly thought of – anyone thinking otherwise would be given short shrift by the soldiers. This dog was special and everyone seemed to see that. Certainly the people of Chateau Thierry were very grateful to the men of the 102nd Infantry, 26th 'Yankee' Division for liberating their beautiful town from the occupying Germans. And as a thank you to the division, the very talented women of the town worked on a special chamois leather coat for Stubby to wear in the cold weather. But the coat was not entirely practical: all over the back and sides the women had sewn or attached the dog's campaign medals, including the Chateau Thierry Campaign Medal, the French Medal of Verdun, St Mihiel Campaign Medal and the Republic of France Grande War Medal. After the war, many other decorations were added to the collection including the Wound Stripe which was replaced with the Purple Heart (America's highest honour for bravery in conflict). But there were two other decorations that were linked by one of Stubby's bravest deeds: the apprehension of a German spy in the US trenches.

It was early morning and the men were woken by a dog barking and howling. Conroy knew that it was his dog making all the commotion. He quickly gathered his rifle and ammunition, as he didn't know what he was going to find, and made his way out of the dugout. There, lying on his face, on the top of the trench, was a German infantryman. His face was turned to the side and he looked ghastly. He must have been terrified out of his wits – he not only had a Bull Terrier standing on his back but Stubby also had a cheek of the man's backside in his jaw. And there was no way on earth he was going to let go! Well, not until the men had gathered themselves together to take control of the prisoner. For this action, Stubby was awarded his three sergeant's stripes for bravery. Much to the delight of his friends and fans worldwide he now outranked his master. In gaining his stripes, Stubby also became the first American dog to take an army rank. The men also thought that the German Iron Cross that he had dangling at the back of the coat was taken from his German prisoner; it seemed the kind of thing that could have happened. But no one knows for sure. And when the medal disappeared off the coat one day it put any worthwhile speculation to bed. But someone, somewhere thought the dog deserved this poetic justice.

After the ladies presented Stubby with his unique coat in the little town of Domrémy (the birthplace of Joan of Arc), the accolades came thick and fast for Stubby. There was hardly any room on the chamois leather coat to take any more. But the dog had fought in seventeen battles in four campaigns and that was quite a feat in itself. The greatest feat was that he survived at all. After completing their hospital visiting duties, it was time for the soldier and the dog to prepare to go home to America.

Although Stubby was well known for his heroic, life-saving deeds Conroy was reluctant to take any chances on the return journey. And so Stubby was smuggled aboard the troop ship the same way he arrived – under the cover of his master's now very torn and weather-beaten greatcoat. It's probable that several officers on duty when the ship docked and when the transfers were made from ship to shore turned a blind eye to the scruffy-looking dog who, like the men, was careworn, battle fatigued and in need of home comforts. No other soldier was going to deny this brave dog his passage home. No one could have that on their conscience.

The end of the war was really just the start of a new life for Stubby. He was destined to be the most decorated dog in America and, no doubt, the world. A well-wisher had added his sergeant's stripes to the now famous coat. They had been sewn right alongside his 'Yankee' Division patch, which was probably the most treasured decoration of all. But the Americans had a greater accolade for this war dog, this champion who raised men's morale in the depths of despair and human destruction. Presented to General 'Black Jack' Pershing – Supreme Commander of the American Forces during the war – Stubby was on his best behaviour. The world's press was looking for the photograph that would capture the heroic spirit of the First World War: the general and the war dog and Stubby didn't disappoint them. Sitting on a table to elevate him to a position where Pershing could decorate the dog for all to see, Stubby sat still and proud on his haunches as the medal was attached to his collar. He seemed to smile throughout the entire ceremony as if being at the centre of attention was his favourite place in the world. The medal was specially commissioned by the Humane Education Society (the forerunner of today's Humane

Society) and was made of gold bearing a simple inscription: 'Stubby'.

In his capacity as returned war hero, Stubby met three US Presidents: Wilson, Harding and Coolidge, who all treated the dog with the same respect the soldiers showed, especially when he saluted them in his own special way. The dog had become as much a soldier as he was still a dog but there were certain canine things he could never be denied. The YMCA gave him lifetime membership plus three bones a day and a place to sleep for the rest of his life. He continued to help his old friends, the American Red Cross with recruiting campaigns and sales of Victory Bonds. As a lifetime member of the American Legion, he marched in every legion parade and attended every convention from the end of the war until his death.

Stubby was never going to need the three bones a day from the YMCA because he was heading home with his master, Private James Robert Conroy. When Conroy decided to study law at Georgetown University, Stubby went along too and in no time was mascot of the football team. He devised his own half-time show, nudging the ball along with his nose and having great fun along the way!

This great American hero passed away in 1926 and the *New York Times* published an obituary that was three columns wide by half a page long. Not many human notables managed to command so many column inches, especially in death.

A nation had taken this brave little battler to their hearts and didn't really want to let him go. Monuments and statues were erected in his honour. The famous painting of the war dog by Charles Ayer Whipple still hangs in the regimental museum in New Haven. Most poignant of all perhaps, for those who, like his devoted master, wanted him to have a continuing presence for all to share, the remains of Stubby are on display at the Smithsonian Institution in Washington D.C. Museum. His coat is perfectly preserved.

Maybe Stubby's story says everything about a generation of young men sent to war to face the enemy knowing that millions of their counterparts had fallen before them. He was brave as they wanted to be brave. He protected his division as many others protected their own in battle. The Hotel Majestic lifted their ban on dogs for just one day. And that day was Stubby's. Stubby was a hero, he was an inspiration but most of all, he was a dog.

Afterword

'Nothing great is easy.' Captain Matthew Webb was said to utter these words in 1875 after becoming the first person to swim the English Channel. If dogs could talk I'm sure those who have accompanied Servicemen and women into war would echo his sentiments. The focus and dedication any person or animal requires to survive adversity in any quantity can sometimes defy belief. Survival is often the prize for those prepared to go beyond the call of duty.

The partnership of Czech airman Václav Robert Bozděch and Antis, the Alsatian puppy he rescued from the ruins of a French farmhouse, extended beyond the conflict of WWII. Trapped by political intrigue in post-war Czechoslovakia, Bozděch was forced to flee his homeland to safeguard his family. He could take only one thing with him – the dog he had saved and who had flown at his feet in a Wellington bomber. Antis remained his only link with his old and new life and his friend and protector until death.

A dog can be one of the most entertaining distractions from the grim reality of war. And the chances of meeting such a loving and faithful companion when surrounded by fear and devastation must carry odds of millions to one. But luck was definitely on the side of a tiny Yorkshire terrier who somehow found herself in the centre of the war in the Pacific and then, miraculously, in the hands of US soldier, Bill Wynne. Smoky's story could have been cut brutally short. But instead, thanks to her saviour, it was one of luck, survival, protection, heroism and lifelong devotion.

Not every dog is cut out for active service and most, like Tangye, fall into it because they like being close to soldiers. From the dog's perspective, the relationship could be based on the quality of the rations and the fuss and attention handed out. From the soldiers' side it's because so many cannot bear to see a helpless creature become a victim of cruel circumstances or culture. And so it was that Tangye, a native Afghan pup, was rescued by British soldiers and taken to their hearts – and then taken home to the UK. His fearlessness in battle was rewarded with freedom.

War has always been fought between nations, and dogs have always been included in the ranks. As companion or protector, Service 'equipment' or mascot, the dog will always give more of itself that first meets the eye. A dog will always give you more than any person could promise in courage, loyalty and love. A dog will always give greatly and go beyond the call of duty.

Bibliography

Farthing, Pen. *One Dog at a Time*, Ebury Press, 2009

Le Chêne, Evelyn. *Silent Heroes*, Souvenir Press, 1994

Richardson, Anthony. *One Man and His Dog*, Harrap, 1960

Ross, Hamish. *Freedom in the Air*, Pen and Sword, 2007

St Hill Bourne, Dorothy. *They Also Serve*, Winchester Publications, 1957

Wynne, William A. *Yorkie Doodle Dandy* – A Memoir, Wynnesome Press, 1996